"The Black Seminole saga is the most important untold story in American history...The U.S. Army fought a war with escaped [formerly enslaved Africans]10 years before the Civil War, and they could not defeat them."

Joseph A. Opala
Former scholar in residence
Penn Center, South Carolina
Adjunct Professor of History
James Madison University, Virginia

THE INVISIBLE WAR

**The African American Anti-Slavery Resistance
from the Stono Rebellion
through the Seminole Wars**

edited by
Y. N. Kly

Clarity Press, Inc.

© 2006 Clarity Press, Inc.
Second printing 2008

ISBN: 0-932863-50-7
  978-0-932863-50-8

In-house editor: Diana G. Collier

Cover photo: **"Assault on Fort Mose"** a Florida National Guard painting by Jackson Walker. Courtesy of the Florida National Guard.

Library of Congress Cataloging-in-Publication Data

The invisible war : the African American war of liberation, 1739-1858 / edited by Y.N. Kly.
    v. cm.
  Contents: Last Stand at Negro Fort / Rodger Lyle Brown—The Gullah War : 1739-1858 / Y.N. Kly —"'Twas a Negro who taught them" : a new look at African labour in early South Carolina / Peter H. Wood — Hidden Muslim Presence in Early African American History : oral history from Gullah-Geechee Elder Cornelia Bailey / interviewed by Carlie Towne — Gullah-Geechee question & answer / based on research by J. Vernon Cromartie.
    ISBN 0-932863-50-7
1. African Americans—Southern States—History—18th century. 2. African Americans—Southern States—History—19th century. 3. African Americans—Southern States—Historiography. 4. Africans—Colonization—Southern States—History. 5. Gullahs—History. 6. Slave insurrections—Southern States—History. 7. Government, Resistance to—Southern States—History. 8. Seminole Indians—Wars. 9. Southern States—History, Military. 10. Southern States—Race relations. I. Kly, Yussuf Naim, 1935-
    E185.I59 2006
    306.3'620896073075—dc22
                        2006011019

CLARITY PRESS, INC.
Ste. 469, 3277 Roswell Rd. NE
Atlanta, GA. 30305
http://www.claritypress.com

TABLE OF CONTENTS

TABLE OF ILLUSTRATIONS

69   **Drawing of a chickee and lithograph of a Seminole town circa 1835.** The drawing is from Clayton MacCauley's 1887 report, *The Seminole Indians of Florida*. Lithograph from the Gray & James series on the war, published in 1837, *courtesy of Star-Banner.com.*

82   **General Jesup.** Engraving, n.d., Florida Photographic Collection. Chromolithograph, 1850-1900, Library of Congress.

119   **Gullah Elder Lisa Wineglass Smalls, Gullah Elders Halim Gullahbemi and Carlie Towne.** (Photo of Halim Gullahbemi and Carlie Towne by Jim French, owner of the African American newspaper, *The Chronicle*.)

73   **Hon. Joshua R. Giddings of Ohio.** Photograph, 1855-1863, Library of Congress.

14, 73   **John Horse, as he appeared around 1840.** Source of the original sketch unknown. The engraving, entitled "Gopher John Seminole Interpreter," first appeared in Sprague's 1848 history of the war, attributed to the firm of N. Orr & Richardson.

143   Detail of **John Horse**, from the engraving by N. Orr in Joshua Giddings' 1858 history, *The Exiles of Florida*.

138   **John Jefferson, John Horse's grandson.** Photograph, 1902, New York Public Library's Schomburg Center for Research in Black Culture

73   **Major Gen. Jackson** circa 1820, from an engraving by James Barton Longacre. *Library of Congress, Prints and Photographs Division, LC-USZ62-435 DLC.*

44   Detail of a **Map of St. Augustine showing the position of Fort Mose ("Fuerte Negro") on the outskirts of the city.** Map created in 1783 by Tomás López de Vargas Machuca. *Library of Congress, Geography and Map Division, G3934.S2 1783 .L6 Vault.*

15   **Map showing Low Country population.** Gullah/Geechee Special Rseource Study Report, National Park Service, December 2003.

79   **"Massacre of Major Dade and his Command,"** engraving depicting Hitchcock's discovery of the Dade battleground, published in 1847 in Barber's *Incidents in American History.*

145   **Micanopy.** Hand-colored lithograph from the McKenney-Hall *History of the Indian tribes of North America* (1858), after an 1825 painting from life by Charles Bird King.

138   Photograph, **Mounted Black Seminole Detachment**, Institute of Texan Cultures 95-369. http://www.texancultures.utsa.edu/seminole/lastwarriors.htm

ACKNOWLEDGMENTS

We wish to salute the website Rebellion: John Horse and the Black Seminoles, First Black Rebels to Beat American Slavery, 2005 <http://www.johnhorse.com>, and its author and producer, Professor J.B. Bird of the University of Texas. The Rebellion website is exemplary, not only for its compilation of existing historical research, its original contributions, and its organization of a large array of scholarly materials, but also for the perspective which it brings to bear on the struggle of forced African immigrants to resist, defy and overthrow the American colonial enslavement system.

The Rebellion website was a primary photo research resource for the illustrations which appear in *The Invisible War*.

"The Gullah War: 1739-1858" by Y.N. Kly first appeared in *The Legacy of Ibo Landing: Gullah Roots of African American Culture*, edited by Marquetta L. Goodwine, published by Clarity Press, Inc. in 1998.

DEDICATION

This book is dedicated to my mother
Mrs. Annie Green
the first South Carolinean folk novelist
and a graduate of Voorhees College.

May God be pleased with her.

Map Showing Low Country Population.
By 1790, Low Country population was 78% Gullah-Geechee. The black majority in South Carolina and Georgia continued well into the 20th Century.

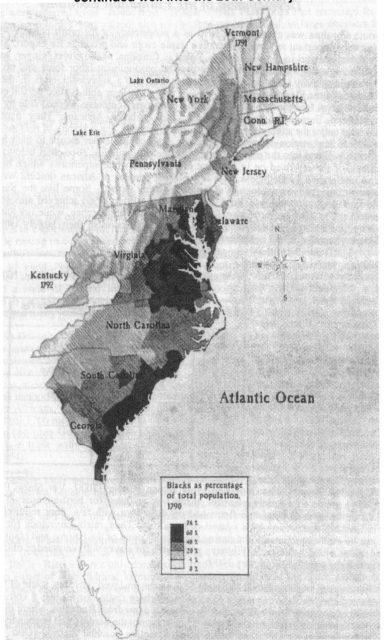

Blacks as percentage
of total population.
1790

78 %
60 %
40 %
20 %
4 %
0 %

PREFACE

This book will raise significant questions concerning central misconceptions related to the enslavement period which are still largely accepted by American historiography:

- That collective resistance to the enslavement system by captured Africans was negligible.

- That self-liberated Africans mostly fled northward to freedom, rather than southward to the free territories of Georgia and Florida.

- That the Seminole Wars were simply another set of Indian wars, rather than wars which marked the collective African resistance to the enslavement system as well.

- That many records of the period (official documents, newspaper records, etc.) were accurate descriptions of fact, rather than censored materials produced in wartime, with a view to enhancing public support and calming public fears.

This book seeks to serve as an instrument to impel thinkers and scholars to revisit this historical period, to seek out and recover this important part of American and African-American history that has been distorted or ignored, due to colonial America's need to be seen in a manner that would attract and morally unify settlers from the various European nations whom it solicited to the new world, and to maintain dominance over those peoples whom it had dispossessed or captured.

In readdressing this historical period, it will be necessary to keep in mind that during this period, there was a savage grab for Indian land and for African labor, and that both these activities had to be not only legitimized but sustained. For such reasons, African-Americans were portrayed as non-humans who benefited from enslavement, and First Nations were portrayed as savages.

Exactly what did the Africans do in response to being taken

captive? Of course, they sought freedom, regardless of where or how it was offered: by the Spanish in Spanish Florida at first, and later by the promises of the Yankees—by any means necessary. They allied with those with whom they could make common cause: the English who sought their help to prevent the American settlers from securing self-determination; the Spanish, who solicited their assistance to prevent the colonists from overrunning Spanish Florida, and of course, with the most natural of their allies, the equally oppressed and aggrieved indigenous First Nations.

The "flight" of hapless individuals, shepherded by courageous guides, to "freedom" in the northern U.S. and Canada has been magnified out of all proportion as the primary manifestation of African-American resistance to captivity. Who has not heard of Harriet Tubman? Of Sojourner Truth? Of John Brown and the other abolitionists? But who has heard of the leaders and fighters of the resisting Africans who fled, not north, but south? Who challenged the system, rather than merely escaping it? Who has heard of **Garçon, the commander who battled forces sent by Andrew Jackson at Negro Fort in Spanish Florida**? Or of Abraham [Ibrahim], John Horse, or Billy Bowlegs, **leaders in the Seminole Wars**? Who knows the real truth of the Indian warrior, Osceola, who was supported by Africans, or the Creek Red Sticks?

Disguised as Indian wars (the Seminole Wars) in the official documents and newspaper reports of the victors, the captured Africans' anti-colonial war of liberation was waged from the free territories of the South, and threatened the hold of what was then a numerical minority of Europeans resting fearfully atop an expansive enslavement system trembling with acts of revolt, large and small, real and imagined.

Who were the Seminoles? While the term first referred to so-called runaways (Africans self-liberated from enslavement and Creek Indians who fled into Florida after the defeat of the Creek Federation), its meaning changed over time to suit the orientation of those who were speaking about the Seminoles' situation. Over time, the existence of the sizeable African component in that entity was downplayed, leading many to believe or claim that Seminoles were an historic Indian culture, the same as any other. But historically, and in the beginning, the Seminoles were both Africans and Indians who together resisted the ongoing expansion of the colonies and their system of enslavement.

Even though the Anglo-American writing of American history has recorded the egregious conditions of enslavement and repudiated that system along with apartheid, the discipline has failed to bring a new consciousness to bear on these past events, reflected in a new lexicon ("captured or enslaved Africans", not "slaves"; "liberated" not "runaway", "African resistance/liberation struggles", not "slave revolts"), and grounded in new political paradigms that reflect the actual and legitimate interpretation and expression of African peoples in relation to the historical events that beset them.

Why should the Africans who liberated themselves from captivity in the American colonies even today be referred to in books as "runaways"—maintaining that term's orientation to their bondage as a legitimate condition, with the "runaway" implicitly a scurrilous wrongdoer rather than a liberated African whose struggle for freedom should be applauded by all who value that ideal? From a culturally neutral perspective, the captured Africans no more became "runaways" than they had been "slaves", and their so-called "masters" were in actuality little more than "kidnappers".

While referring to the records of the past, contemporary historiography still thoughtlessly adopts and transmits such references as "masters", and "was owned by". This is vicious in the sense that it is intentional, and savage in the sense that it ignores the full individual, cultural and collective humanity of the captured Africans, and thereby of their descendants.

African-American history as written largely remains a political history which has admitted the historical flow of systemic change (from enslavement to apartheid to civil rights/nondiscrimination in the modern period) without challenging the domination of the Anglo-American perspective on it (his-story). In short, we still talk about the African American past as if we do not know that the African-American not only is, but also was in the past, a human being with human dignity and human rights.

Even when the Africans' simple humanity could no longer be effectively denied, the new historians, greatly influenced by the emerging abolitionist movement, once again wrote African American history—this time to prove African-American humanity on the basis of the Africans' ability to adapt to Anglo-American cultural and educational norms, as if they were simply the same as Anglo-Americans. Of course, for Africans to have values and cultures in any manner different from the Anglo-Americans was considered as "proof" of their savagery, and was initially forbidden by the law of the Black Codes.

This book seeks to solicit historians and political scientists to unravel the factual record of what captured Africans actually did. It begins with a contribution by Rodger Lyle Brown which explores the circumstances surrounding the historic confrontation between the Africans and colonists in Spanish Florida at what came to be known as Negro Fort. No doubt the first Seminole War set the stage and circumstances for the Second and Third Seminole Wars.

The second article,"The Gullah War", provides a glimpse into what happened after Negro Fort. Drawing heavily on first hand observation and documentation of the abolitionists, it revisits what is presently known as the Seminole Wars to highlight the participation and leadership roles assumed by the African forced immigrants (the United Nations Special Rapporteur's term, used interchangeably here with captive Africans and Gullah to designate the original African population that was forcibly emigrated to America), and the gravity of the threat posed by communities of free Africans in the south to the colonial enslavement system,

The third article is by historian Peter H. Woods, whose groundbreaking work first challenged the depiction of the forcibly emigrated African population as ignorant and helpless.It also reveals the strategic situation and position of the captured Africans in relation to their ability to resist, by demonstrating the various competencies of the captured Africans. Their greater knowledge of the geographic conditions into which their captors introduced them, and their relative expertise in matters related to travel, cultivation, language skills, and survival in general, makes an implicit point: the African population, which for a period of time was a numerical majority, had the capacity to mount a successful anti-colonial resistance.

"The Hidden Presence of Muslims in Early African American History," is an interview conducted with Gullah-Geechee Elder Cornelia Bailey at her home on Sapelo Island. A descendant of Bilali, one of the best known among the African Muslim captives to first arrive in America, Cornelia Bailey exemplifies the African tradition of oral history by providing invaluable recollections concerning the early experiences of Africans in colonial America, and most strikingly, on how they sheltered and maintained their Islamic faith, even as it was channeled through forced assimilation into the Christian religion.

A "Gullah-Geechee Question and Answer" follows, based on the research of Gullah historian, J. Vernon Cromartie. It seeks to introduce readers to the collective culture of the first Africans to form communities in the U.S., and to highlight and celebrate the African and Native American forebears who struggled together against the colonial system.

The final chapter registers the Library of Congress war records to verify the capture of African Americans after and during their resistance by the U.S. Army, particularly under the leadership of Andrew Jackson, etc., with a view to commemorating the brave and honorable heroes of the Gullah-Geechee and African-American anti-enslavement resistance who dedicated their lives to the ideal also articulated in the American Declaration of Independence: that all men are created equal and endowed by their Creator with certain inalienable rights, among which are life, liberty and the pursuit of happiness.

We hope that you will enjoy reading *The Invisible War,* and perhaps come to better understand the invisible historical heritage of the U.S. that so often suddenly materializes—or disappears! We hope that you will keep vigilant watch over the recording of contemporary African-American experience, and even over the existing and acknowledged records of earlier periods.

In particular, we point to the increasing historical invisibility of the Reconstruction period and the gradual removal of public awareness of its Afro-Carolinian-dominated democratic government from our historical consciousness—perhaps due in no small part to the highly progressive nature of the government that came into being under African-American leadership. Though it was quickly snuffed out, as President Andrew Johnson facilitated the efforts of the Confederacy *ancien regime* to re-establish white supremacy, the historical record of the nondiscriminatory and progressive policies of an African-American-led government remains, and should be remembered, protected, and preserved as a legacy to future generations.

With the advent of an African American presently contending for the presidency of the United States, there is much hope for a real change in the African American slave orientation of the U.S. vision. However, if this change does not occur as a normal result of African decolonization and consequential greater visibility in the world, For the African Americans, the pertinent question is whether it is the end of the effort to enslave them, or the continuation of this historical process.

The forced use of African people as the raw material for the animation of the U.S. capitalistic economic system was no doubt a difficult endeavor, adventure and dangerous experiment, probably as complex as putting a man on the moon. It required several obvious conditions:

Stage One:
1) First, proclaiming to an isolated and therefore globally ig-
    norant European population that the Africans were an un-
    civilized sub-human people who could be trained to accept
    enslavement and to provide children who would do the same.
2) The separation and isolation of a group of individual Afri-
    cans from their various cultures, and their various languages,

in such a manner that they would be unable (for a sufficient amount of time) to communicate with each other, and would be obliged to adopt the oppressor's language, etc., even in communications with each other (note the prisons of Elmina in Ghana and Isle de Gore in Senegal and the early pest and cabin houses in South Carolina, etc.

3) The discovery of and conquest of such a land where such an experiment in chattel slavery might take place.

4) The children of the candidates for slavery had to be taught at first that they had no history, culture or language, that as such, they were not fully human beings, and that they belonged to their oppressors.

5) When they revolted against this nonsense, they had to be convinced, as Condoleeza Rice and her president, George Bush often implied when dealing with the Palestinians, that "to resist is useless", and "Do what you are told, or die and go to hell for resisting". (This involved the role of the Black Church.)

6) When they still resisted, they had to be killed or imprisoned. All records of successful revolts or wars were downplayed or ignored, with the attempt to obliterate such events from being recorded in history, and thereby accessible to succeeding generations to inspire their struggles for justice.

7) When the revolts of Africans began to be difficult to stop, it soon became necessary to legally admit their humanity and force them into accepting voluntary servitude. To do this required that the oppressor convince the Africans that they had been emancipated by the great and benevolent oppressor, Abraham Lincoln. Now they expect great reward for their forced labor and redress for the oppressors' crimes against humanity—as well as the right to say that they, too, are human beings.

Stage Two

1) When it appeared that African Americans had learned the hard way how to be satisfied with just being able to say the obvious: that they are human beings. They could now be able to live (culturally) according to the oppressor's definition of human beings.

2) As human beings as defined by the oppressor, they could now live in segregated communities, learning how to perform voluntary servitude and aping the Anglo-Americans as

being the only culture of human beings.

3) When the African Americans refused to accept this arrangement for voluntary servitude (slavery), several solutions (by the African American community) were offered. The most popular were return to Africa, desegregation, and separate but equal nations within the U.S. state However, the government opted for a form of forced assimilation solution (based on the obvious understanding that given historical, politico-cultural, economic, and socio-psychological, etc. advantages, that the Anglo American (white) ethny had over the African American ethny, that the latter would have no other choice than to accept voluntary servitude or die in attempting to express their need to be recognized as different.

4) This governmental option (different from the peoples of the colonies) would also prevent the African American people from achieving the socio-economic development of African Americans by not providing them with the political space to attend to their own unique socio-political needs, and from achieving international recognition as a people or nation, or a separate and equal status community. They could now be forever treated as a social minority whose difficulties in achieving equal status benefits resulted from some form of socio-economic or intellectual retardation.

5) Each step of the great American experiment acts in the real world to continue to victimize the African American, placing them in socio-political and economic situations where they must always play by the rules of their oppressors, never being able to create new rules, etc. that might be necessary for the development of their own collective circumstances and evolving situations (no political or legal free choice that is specifically focused on their needs as a people), no matter how important or necessary this might be for the victims' own development.

6) In this sense, the African American can still be said to belong to the American oppressors, not in the sense of being in the same country, but in the physical sense as well, like a table or a chair, etc.

When we speak of African American history, it usually has three specificities:

1) The Anglo-American history of African-American relations with them.

2) The history of the shortcomings or successes of the African American efforts to imitate the socio-cultural and political models of the Anglo-Americans (whites).

3) The full history of the efforts of African American people themselves to resolve their problems within the framework of their recent popular movements and efforts.

    a.   During each period of African American history, such efforts occurred but failed and were ignored by government. (Compare Booker T. Washington with Marcus Garvey, the leadership of Martin Luther King with that of Elijah Muhammad, Malcolm X, etc.

    b.   This same failure to win politically and being ignored was always the significant feature of African Americans' history where popular movements of African Americans strove to achieve the goals and freedom of their people within the framework of their own desires and understanding.

This book is a scholarly effort to present the facts and events of one of these ignored but most important liberation efforts.

RECONSTRUCTION:
An African American Majority in the South Carolina Legislature

Radical Members of the First Legislature after the War, South Carolina. Photograph. 1878. A scant twenty years after the Gullah anti-enslavement resistance might be viewed to have "ended", and following upon their heroic effort in the US civil war, an African American-dominated legislature came into being in South Carolina. Does it make sense to view this new political institutionalization as a sudden Anglo-American embrace of a servile African population, or even simply as Northern gratitude to a wartime ally? Might it not be as accurately viewed as the victorious fruit of the forced African immigrant population's historic century-long resistance to their American colonial capitivity for the purposes of forced labor?

1st South Carolina Volunteer Infantry, 1862-1863
by Don Troiani

CHAPTER ONE

A STAND FOR FREEDOM
The Story of Negro Fort

Rodger Lyle Brown

They were an army of African[1] shock troops, recruited from escapees who had been enslaved and now lived in Spanish Florida. They had been trained by the British as Colonial Marines for a possible invasion of the United States. The plan was to tie down American fighting forces in Georgia, threaten a slave rebellion across the South, and help bring the British a victory in the War of 1812. Their reward would be freedom and land of their own.

But it never happened. The war ended. The British withdrew. At one moment poised to help liberate the Africans enslaved in the United States and restore Indian lands seized by Andrew Jackson at the end of the bloody Creek War, the army of escapees, under the command of a 30-year-old former slave carpenter named Garson,[2] was abandoned by all its allies. The British sailed away. The Red Stick Creeks, who had prepared to fight alongside the escapees, drifted back to their towns and villages.

The African fighters, numbering from 100 to 150, along with nearly 200 women and children, were left alone in the thick Florida forest. They were left alone, but they were not left helpless. The British left them with cannon, muskets, swords and thousands of

---

[1] While the exact genealogies of most of the British recruits and other occupants of Negro Fort aren't known, "African" is used here as collective reference for the enslaved and formerly enslaved in this story in order to give them a collective representation similar to the other diverse yet collectively represented "national" players on the scene such as the "British," the "Americans," etc. There is additional justification for this besides just apparent racial categories. Patrick Riordan. "Finding Freedom in Florida: Native Peoples, African Americans, and Colonists, 1670-1816. *Florida Historical Quarterly*. Vol. 75; No. 1. Summer 1996.

[2] His name also appears in various sources as Garzon and Garçon, French for "boy".

pounds of gunpowder, all stockpiled in a virtually impregnable fortress built on a high bluff 15 miles up the Apalachicola River from the Gulf of Mexico.[3]

The site commanded views up and down the wide, slow, shallow meander. It had been a crossroads visited seasonally by native people during hunting trips, but was never the site of a permanent settlement until British traders had built a store there around 1804. And it had been a relatively quiet place until the British sent their Royal Marines up the river in 1814 as part of a grand campaign to crush the ambitions of the young United States. Creek and Seminole Indians called the place Achackweithle. The Spanish called it Loma de Buenavista. English speakers called it Prospect Bluff. British Colonel Edward Nicolls, who directed the construction of the fortification there, called it "the British post on the Apalachicola." After Nicolls withdrew and, as John Quincy Adams described it a short time later, "took with him the white portion of his force" leaving the massive arms cache to "the negro department of his allies," word spread quickly throughout the southeast that there was an army of black soldiers in possession of cannon, powder, muskets and swords, who were declaring themselves free at a place now called Negro Fort.

It was a simple, descriptive name, but it contained within it all the fear and dread of insurrection and uprising that had haunted the sleep of slave owners throughout Georgia and the Carolinas, especially since a vicious and bloody slave rebellion in the Caribbean had given birth to the Republic of Haiti little more than a decade earlier. Tales of the torture and slaughter of slaveholders on Santo Domingo, as well as the defeat of Spanish, British and French forces by African fighters, had horrified southern slave owners. Now there was an African army just a few dozen miles from American plantations.[4] For the erstwhile owners of the enslaved Africans, as well as those who still kept men and women in bondage, Negro Fort

---

[3] The actual number is in dispute. At the end of 1814, one visitor estimate around 500 blacks and Indians combined occupied the site. The next year, another estimated 450 blacks and 800-900 Indians were in the area with people coming and going frequently until American and Allied Creek forces began to move against the fort. The consensus has been that between 300- 400 people occupied the fort in July 1816, but Claudio Saunt has questioned that. See Claudio Saunt, *A New Order of Things*. Cambridge University Press. 2009. Pp. 281-282.

[4] John Quincy Adams to George W. Erving. Nov. 28, 1818. American State Papers. Foreign Relations. 540.

was the physical manifestation of a persistent nightmare of the enslaver—the fear of black insurrection, rebellion, and righteous vengeance.

The fort's walls were 15 feet high and 18 feet thick. Its earthen parapet was 120 feet in diameter and was surrounded by a moat 14 feet wide and four feet deep. Heavy artillery lined its walls. With a thick swamp to its rear and streams to the north and south, it was considered virtually invulnerable to any land-based attack. Although it was located in sovereign territory claimed by Spain, Garson and his men flew the Union Jack as their standard, and many wore the red coats given them by the British Royal Marines. News that the fort was under the control of an army of liberated slaves spread through slave quarters throughout the southeast, and eventually the number of fugitives making their way to the countryside around the fort grew to an estimated high of 800. The number of armed men occupying the fort spread panic and alarm throughout the south. "From this spot they can easily annoy our settlements on the Flint river and the whole Georgia frontier, and are in a country where they can procure subsistence with facility," an officer later described the situation to Gen. Andrew Jackson.[5]

Confident and hopeful, the free African settlers planted fields of pumpkins and corn for 50 miles along the banks of the Apalachicola. A village grew up under the protection of the fort and its black soldiers. Herds of cattle grazed in the forests.

It was the spring of 1815. Garson and his people had a year to live.

For nearly two centuries, the story of Negro Fort on the Apalachicola has been treated as an historical footnote in many histories: the British campaign in the Gulf during the War of 1812; the Creek War; the decline of Spanish rule on the mainland east of the Mississippi; the hagiographies of Andrew Jackson; the beginning of the Seminole wars. In most instances, it's viewed as an anomaly, an accident of circumstance and coincidence. In the traditional historical narratives of early American history, enslaved African men and women appear as obstacles, impediments, objects posing an unreasoning danger or possessions of value and bounty. Looked at

---

[5] Amelung to Gen. Andrew Jackson. June 4, 1816. American State Papers. Foreign Relations. 557.

in a broader context, however, the brief glory and sudden tragedy of Negro Fort can be seen not simply as an oddity and strange exception within the grand struggles among imperial powers for land and power; rather, the story of Negro Fort is a dramatic example of the persistent impulse for liberty among many of the enslaved Africans who, when given the opportunity—as well as the arms and munitions—chose to sacrifice their lives in concerted acts of collective resistance throughout the history of slavery in North America. Historical circumstance might have brought Africans escaping enslavement to Negro Fort, but it was their will to freedom that led them to make a stand there and declare that they would never surrender.

Due to the predominance of the antebellum and Civil War periods as subjects of popular history, most contemporary readers think "runaway slaves" in the South always ran north when they sought to escape bondage. That's not true. Africans escaping enslavement began running to Spanish Florida almost as soon as the peculiar institution appeared on the continent. Before the U.S. finally took Florida from Spain in 1821, escapees seeking freedom from slaveholders in Georgia and South Carolina kept the rising sun on their left. Balancing this historical bias serves well to highlight more of the fluid contingencies that ultimately helped shape the forms American slavery took as the country moved inexorably toward Civil War. The military actions in which free Africans took part during both the first and second Spanish periods in Florida also helped people the nightmares that haunted the sleep of slave owners.

The first known instance of Africans fleeing enslavement in an English settlement for sanctuary among the Spanish in Florida occurred in 1687 when eight men, two women and a nursing child sailed into St. Augustine and asked for refuge. This was only 17 years after the frigate *Carolina* made landfall up the river from Charleston Harbor bringing the first enslaved Africans into the low country. The Spanish themselves kept slaves and had their own legacy of brutality—from the Black Legend from the age of conquest to the torturous practices of the Inquisition—but the continual need for soldiers and laborers in Florida compelled them to evolve an official policy of offering sanctuary to those who escaped from the English slaveholders, made it across the border, pledged loyalty to the crown, converted to Catholicism and agreed to pick up a gun and serve in the local militia.

By the 1730s, the population of free Africans in Florida had become a significant part of the population and a key component in Spain's defense of its steadily eroding claim on the territory it had first named *La Florida*, the Land of Flowers. The lure of Florida to Africans enslaved in the colonies was dramatically displayed in September 1739 when a group of them near Stono in South Carolina rose up, and, waving banners, beating drums and chanting "*Freedom!*" began fighting their way toward Florida, leaving houses in flames and two dozen whites dead before being stopped by Carolina militia.

For more than 100 years, Florida was the main destination for escapees after King Charles II of Spain had proclaimed a policy of offering sanctuary in 1693, "giving liberty to all...the men as well as the women...so that by their example and by my liberality others will do the same..."[6] The policy wasn't purely altruistic of course; the escapees deprived the British of scarce labor and delivered that resource to the labor-starved Spanish. The English colonists felt the pain. In 1740, one colonist wrote:

> It is with great Reason, we apprehend, that that Part of our Calamities, proceeding from the frequent Attempts of our Slaves, arises from the Designs and Intrigues of our Enemies the Spaniards in St. Augustine and Florida, who have had the Ruin and Destruction of your Majesty's Colonies of South Carolina and Georgia long in View...[M]any have already deserted, and others encouraged daily to do the same; and even those who have committed the most inhuman Murders, are there harboured, entertained and caressed.[7]

By the turn of the 19th century, much had changed. The British had taken control of Florida from Spain at the end of the Seven Years War in 1763 and administered it as two colonies, East

---

[6] Jane Landers. "Cimmarron Ethnicity and Cultural Adaptation in the Spanish Domains of the CircumCaribbean, 1503-1763. pp. 30-54. in, Paul E. Lovejoy, *Identity in the Shadow of* Slavery. Continuum International Publishing Group. 2000.

[7] Petition to the King. July 26, 1740. The Egmont Papers. Vol. 14205, Letters from Georgia, June 1740-June 1741. Hargrett Rare Book and Manuscript Library. University of Georgia. Athens, Ga.

Florida and West Florida (hence the frequent references to 'the Floridas'). During the next two decades, the territory was shut off as a refuge for escapees although numerous earlier African escapees still lived in the countryside in mutually agreeable relationships with the Seminole Indians. The two British Florida colonies did not join the original 13 rebellious colonies, so when the American Revolution ended in 1783, Britain returned the Floridas to Spain. The Spanish once again returned to the mainland east of the Mississippi, but never again posed a serious military threat to the young United States. Spain's global empire was in tatters following the devastation the home country suffered during the Napoleonic era, and its troops were spread thin throughout South America, the Caribbean and the Phillipines.

Florida was no long the vital stronghold it was throughout the 16th and much of the 17th century when forces based there served as a buffer protecting the rich gold and silver mines in Central and South American mines from English and French interlopers. With few of its own soldiers available to station in St. Augustine or Pensacola, Spain in the 18th and early 19th centuries was forced to manage its self-defense any way it could, with any soldiers willing and able to fight. By the time American expansionists launched their first attempt to seize East Florida from the Spanish in 1812 (they'd already successfully seized a chunk of West Florida between the Mississippi and the Perdido Rivers), the eager and cocky self-proclaimed "Patriots of East Florida" marching on St. Augustine learned exactly what that entailed.

"They have armed every able bodied Negro within their power," Georgia Governor David Mitchell wrote with alarm to President Madison and Secretary of State James Monroe as they watched the fumbling efforts of the Patriots from afar, eager to maintain plausible deniability if and when the campaign went awry, lest they be implicated in an illegal invasion of a sovereign nation. "They have also received from the Havanna (sic), reinforcement of nearly two companies of black troops...[If they] are suffered to remain in the province, our southern country will soon be in a state of insurrection."[8]

Mitchell's pleas for assistance repeatedly focused on the

---

[8] David Mitchell to Sec. of State James Monroe, July 17, 1812. Cited in Jane Landers, *Black Society in Spanish Florida*. University of Illinois Press; Chicago. 1999. 222.

Spaniards' use of black fighters. African men in arms posed a serious danger to the fatigued and isolated Patriot militia and the few U.S. forces accompanying them, but they also represented more—a challenge to a social order that was increasingly based on their suppression and conversion into an enslaved workforce. The danger was very real. Africans fighting to defend their freedom and that of their families and their allied supporters needed to be recast in the colonial rhetoric as lawless, undisciplined, brutal bandits—and preferably not even as Africans, at all—hence their inclusion/ submersion under the term "Seminole".[9] They needed to be stopped now, before the apocalypse of black rebellion was visited upon the southern states.

Mitchell cried to Madison and Monroe that the Spanish governor of St. Augustine had:

> proclaimed freedom to every Negro who will join his standard, and has sent a party of them to unite with, and who are actually at this time united with the Indians in their murderous excursions…It is a fact that most of our male Negroes on the seaboard are restless and make many attempts to get to St. Augustine.[10]

Mitchell even claimed that if it weren't for the black fighters, swift victory would have been easy for the Patriots. "Indeed the principal strength of the garrison of St. Augustine consists of Negroes, there being but a few Militia of the Province in the place … and about one hundred effective men, the remains of an old Battalion of Regular Troops, whom it was understood would surrender without firing a shot."[11]

The use of African fighters by the Spanish was so outrageous to Mitchell that he even went so far as to protest to the Spanish that the presence of black troops on the battlefield was somehow unfair,

---

[9] As discussed in Chapter 2, "The African-American Insurgency", by Dr. Y. N. Kly.
[10] Mitchell to Monroe, Sept. 19, 1812. Territorial Papers of the United States Senate 1789-1873. Cited in Dennis Stevenson. "War, Words, and the Southern Way: The Florida Acquisition and the Rhetoric of Southern Honor." PhD dissertation. University of Florida. 2004.
[11] Ibid. 87.

especially given the recent carnage in Santo Domingo and the justifiable fear among Southerners that armed black men might easily spark a similar slave rebellion on the mainland. "Your certain knowledge of the peculiar situation of the southern section of the Union in regard to that description of people [African troops], one might have supposed, would have induced you to abstain from introducing them into the province, or of organizing such as were already in it."[12]

Those free Africans—"such as were already in it"—proved to be much more of a danger to the white invasion than the imported black soldiers from Spain's Caribbean provinces whose reputation as fighters was held in low esteem even by the Spanish governor who has ordered them up. Not only were the Africans good fighters, they were acculturated to life in the sub-tropics of Florida and intimate with the Native American populations. Their influence on the Seminoles was profound. When hostilities first broke out during the Patriot invasion, the Seminoles had decided to stay neutral in the conflict between Americans and Spaniards. Patriot leaders had promised they wouldn't be disturbed, that the fight was between them and the 'Dons." But then a black man named Anthony, considered one of the finest Indian linguists in the region, overheard Patriot boasting and quickly met with Seminole leaders to debunk the Patriots' pacifying claims: "These fine talks are made to amuse you and deceive you," he told them. "They are going to take your country beyond the St. Johns, the old people will be put to sweep the yards of the white people, the young men to work for them, and the young females to spin and weave for them." A Creek interpreter who frequently worked with the southeastern Indian agent, Benjamin Hawkins, reported that Tony's speech did the trick. "After the Indians heard the talk of the Negro they believed it."[13]

As the Patriots' siege of St. Augustine wore on, the U.S. commander in charge sounded a warning that would echo loudly just a few years later after the construction of the Negro Fort: "They [the Seminoles] have...several hundred fugitive slaves from the Carolinas & Georgia at present in their Towns & unless they are

---

[12] David Mitchell to Sebastian Kindelan, July 6, 1812. Cited in Landers, *Black Society in Spanish Florida*. 222.
[13] Robert L. Anderson. "The End of an Idyll," *Florida Historical Quarterly*. Vol 42; No. 1. July 1963. 38.

checked soon they will be so strengthened by [more] desertions from Georgia & Florida…it will be found troublesome to reduce them."[14]

Georgia's Gov. Mitchell also seemed to anticipate what lay in the future if the Madison administration didn't send more support for the invasion. "[I]t would be attended by the most fatal consequences for Georgia, and indeed, nothing short of the whole military strength of the state of Georgia being brought to act against the Indians and negroes, would, in my opinion, save her from the very worst evils imaginable."[15]

With the Patriots frustrated in their attack on St. Augustine, American Maj. Daniel Newnan then planned a punitive campaign into Seminole country to break up the "evil system of Negro villages." Two weeks later, Newnan and his men were trapped, starving and eating their horses. After facing "a considerable reinforcement of negroes and Indians from their towns," Newnan later reported, he and his men barely made it out alive. An observer from Georgia noted that the beaten, bloody men were "burdened with misery and grief." The newspapers nonetheless hailed Newnan's campaign as a heroic victory; it would never do for a white army to be defeated by a band of black men. It was symptomatic of the unreliability of the American media of the day as a resource for research into historical events in relation to the African resistance.

Near hysteria, another Patriot leader directly conjured up the specter of Santo Domingo, the bloody and brutal uprising that led to the creation of the Republic of Haiti.

> Our slaves are excited to rebel, and we have an army of negroes raked up in this country…to contend with. Let us ask, if we are abandoned, what will be the situation of the Southern States, with this body of black men in the neighborhood of St. Augustine, the whole Province will be the refuge of fugitive slaves; and from thence emissaries can, and no doubt will be detached, to bring about a

[14] Lt. Col. Smith to Maj. Gen. Pinckney, July 30, 1812. In T. Frederick Davis, "United States Troops in Spanish East Florida, 1812-1813, Part II." *Florida Historical Quarterly*. Vol. 9; No. 3. Jan. 1931. Pp. 106-107.
[15] Mitchell to Monroe, Oct. 13, 1812. State Papers and Publick Documents of the United States. Vol. IX. 1819. 174-175.

revolt of the black population of the United States. A nation that can stir up the savages round your western frontiers to murder will hesitate but little to introduce the horrors of St. Domingo into your Southern country.[16]

Eventually, the Patriot siege of St. Augustine was broken after a party of Africans and Indians ambushed a supply convoy of U.S. Marines. The Spanish governor at St. Augustine later reported that while most American newspapers (and later historians) would highlight the action as an Indian fight, it was actually an engagement largely fought by the black militia, "our parties of blacks whome they [the Patriots] think are Indians because they wear the same clothing and go painted."[17]

The Spanish remained in control of St. Augustine. All that was left for the American military was a vengeful, retaliatory raid on Seminole country that would finally break the back of the African-Indian alliance. "Every negro found in arms will be put to death without mercy," declared Brigadier General Flournoy as Tennessee cavalrymen dressed in black and carrying knives and tomahawks rode through eastern Florida burning Seminole villages, killing cattle and spoiling food supplies.[18] Hundreds of Seminole Indian homes were torched before they finally asked for peace. Indian agent Hawkins delivered the terms: surrender the blacks who had lived and fought with them for generations. "I will venture to say if [the escapees] are collected and delivered up, it will be considered by Georgia as one of the best evidences of the sincerity of their present proposition for peace," Gov. Mitchell said triumphantly.

Although the Georgians' demands weren't met immediately— the Patriots were recalled and U.S. plans to seize Florida temporarily sidelined—the pressure on the Seminoles to surrender their black compatriots was a harbinger of things to come. The Americans wouldn't quit until the Africans were back in chains. While the Seminoles gathered at new villages in the interior, the African warriors and their families drifted south toward Tampa Bay and west toward

---

[16] Cited in Landers, *Black Society in Spanish Florida*, 222.
[17] Ibid. 226.
[18] Kenneth Porter. *Black Seminoles: History of a Freedom-Seeking People*. University Press of Florida. 1991. 11.

the Suwannee and the Apalachicola. It was the summer of 1813.

It would not be long before the Africans had a chance to fight again. The U.S. had declared war on Great Britain. A civil war had broken out among the Creek Indians occupying what today is western Georgia and eastern Alabama. American settlers and land speculators were pushing against the borders of every frontier. Within two years, these disparate, global forces would culminate in the creation of the most heavily armed, longest-occupied military fortress held by free blacks in U.S. history.

***

North of the scourged Seminole lands in Florida, Indian agent Benjamin Hawkins was aware of the fighting that had taken place around St. Augustine, but he assured officials in Washington that everything was under control in Creek country. In June, he wrote to the Secretary of War, "From the present disposition of the Creeks, there is nothing hostile to be apprehended of them." Hawkins' report of Creek tranquility was largely disingenuous. The largest Indian confederacy in the southeast was being torn apart by conflict between factions that wanted to adopt European-American cultural practices and those who didn't; between those who wanted to resist American encroachment and those who wanted to accommodate them. Two months after Hawkins' misleading report to the secretary of war, Red Stick Creeks (the anti-American faction) massacred hundreds of white, black and mixed-blood settlers and slaves at Fort Mims north of Mobile, turning what had been a smoldering civil war among the Creeks into all-out war with the Americans.

Fort Mims would have been just another episode of violence in Creek country if not for one factor: the fugitive Africans fighting with the Red Sticks. It would have been bloody, would have been brutal, but most likely would not have been the total slaughter that made it the greatest Native American victory over a fortified position in U.S. history if not for the relentless ferocity of the Africans fighting with the Red Sticks. As told by the only Creek Indian who wrote a memoir of the Red Stick War, at one point during the attack on Fort Mims, both sides had fought to a draw. The attacking Red Sticks had taken more casualties than they had anticipated. They were disillusioned and angry that the magic of their religious leaders had not made them invincible to bullets. Their own dead lay everywhere on the field, and survivors inside the stockade were still firing. The Red Sticks began to quit the field.

The African fighters wouldn't let them. As George Stiggins later recalled: "They would not have commenced their attack anew, but the Negroes they had would not cease, urging them on by reciting that they thought it interested them to have the fort destroyed. The Indians were urged on to the charge and renewed the attack."

"The Negroes," he said, wanted to "kill all the white people and be free."[19]

The attack was a tragic success. All but a handful of the occupants of Fort Mims were killed and the stockade burnt. Hundreds of the attacking Red Sticks were also killed and any satisfaction with the victory was short-lived. Within weeks, three American armies were riding into Creek country. For the Creeks—both the Red Sticks and those allied with the Americans—ultimately the war was a disaster. In a series of battles between November 1813 and March 1814, American militia and regular army troops, often fighting in conjunction with allied Creeks, defeated the Red Sticks in one engagement after another. Villages and towns throughout Creek country were burned. Finally the Red Sticks staged a last stand at a place called Horseshoe Bend on the Tallapoosa River. Nearly 1,000 Red Sticks died, with merely a few dozen U.S. deaths. Gen. Andrew Jackson assumed the war was over in Creek country and he quickly forced the Creeks to surrender more than 20 million acres of their prime land—hills, valleys and rivers that would within months begin the transition into the great southern cotton belt.

For about 2,000 Red Stick refugees, however, the war would never end. They migrated south into Spanish Florida and gathered near Pensacola, starving and unarmed, but eager to strike back against the Americans. That was where the British found them. Both sides discovered they shared a mutual goal.

U.S. President James Madison had declared war on Great Britain in June of 1812, and by 1813 the war had virtually stalemated. In 1814, negotiations began in Belgium between the U.S. and Great Britain. British Admiral Alexander Cochrane, however, was anxious to launch an attack on the Gulf coast before any treaty was signed

[19] George Stiggins. *Creek Indian History: A Historical Narrative of the Genealogy, Traditions and Downfall of the Ispocoga or Creek Indian Tribe of Indians.* Birmingham Public Library Press; Birmingham. 1989. Pp. 104-105; 112.

with the ultimate goal being seizure of New Orleans and the millions of dollars worth of goods stored on the docks there. Whoever controlled New Orleans, controlled the Mississippi; and whoever controlled the Mississippi, controlled the trade of the entire middle of North America west of the Appalachians. If the British could seize New Orleans before the war was over, they would have effectively stopped American expansion west of the Appalachians.

As Cochrane developed his plans, news reached him of the crushing defeat suffered by the Red Stick Creeks at the hand of Gen. Andrew Jackson at Horseshoe Bend. When Cochrane learned of the thousands of Indians still ready to fight the Americans, he quickly sent contingents of Royal Marines into the territory to feed, arm and train them. While they were at it, he noted, they were also to make a special effort to "encourage the flight of negroes" and promise land and freedom to any slaves who wished to escape their owners and join the British.

By the summer of 1814, British officers were sending optimistic reports back to Admiral Cochrane about the enthusiastic reception given them by the Indians and Africans in the area. Others took note of these activities as well. By mid-summer, Benjamin Hawkins forwarded to the U.S. Secretary of War the news he had picked up from his spies. The British had invited all surviving Red Sticks to join them and "refresh themselves" with arms and ammunition, he said. They were recruiting black slaves and inciting others to run away and enlist. British Colonel Edward "Fighting" Nicolls had aggressively followed Cochrane's suggestion to liberate slaves in the area and recruit them into his force, and had instructed the Red Sticks in the area to spread the word north and encourage "by every means the emigration of Negroes from Georgia and the Carolinas." The Red Sticks promised Nicolls they would "get all the black men we can."[20]

Soon, formerly-enslaved Africans from Georgia and the Carolinas were coming into Florida by the dozens. Hawkins wrote, "They are training the Indians and some negroes for purposes hostile to us." Nicolls could have been commenting on much of the combat that had taken place in the previous few years from St. Augustine to Fort Mims when he wrote to Admiral Cochrane that the "Indians and blacks are very good friends and cooperate bravely together."[21]

---

[20] Saunt,*A New Order of Things*. 278.
[21] Saunt,*A New Order of Things*. 278.

By the fall, Nicolls had taken control of Spanish Pensacola with 100 Royal Marines and an estimated 600 Indians and blacks. Jackson was anticipating a major British assault somewhere in the Gulf, and in November he quickly moved to drive Nicolls and his force out of the town. Ill-prepared to face Jackson's troops, Nicolls withdrew to Prospect Bluff where, by the beginning of 1815, nearly 3,000 men, women and children had gathered at the site where a massive fortification was under construction.

The British colonel in charge of "the British post on the Apalachicola," Edward Nicolls, was a veteran of the Napoleonic wars and one of Cochrane's best field officers. An anonymous correspondent described him to Andrew Jackson as "an impatient blustering Irishman…apparently brave and cruel." British Secretary of State for War and the Colonies, Earl Bathurst, described him to American ambassador John Quincy Adams as "a man of activity and spirit, but a very wild fellow."[22] Nicolls had such a wild spirit that despite personally witnessing the slaughter of British troops at New Orleans and losing an eye during that ill-fated invasion, he refused to abandon his fort on the Apalachicola, or his Indian allies and his black recruits, even after receiving word in February 1815 that the Treaty of Ghent had been signed and the war was over.

For months Nicolls held to the position that Article 9 of the treaty obliged the Americans to return all Indian lands that had been taken during the war and to reinstate the boundaries as they existed in 1812. To him, that meant returning the millions of acres the Creeks lost in the Treaty of Fort Jackson. The Americans, of course, had a different interpretation, claiming the treaty with the Creeks had been signed before the Treaty of Ghent, and therefore Article 9 did not apply. By May, Nicolls was finally forced to leave Florida and take his case to London where he hoped to convince the authorities to agree to a treaty with the Creeks that would obligate Great Britain to defend their claim to their lost lands. It would be a futile venture.

At the fort, with the British gone, the mood was grim and determined. At the end of 1814, a Spanish officer sent to Prospect Bluff to gather them up reported that other than a handful of women and children, most of the Africans refused to leave, protesting that

---

[22] Extract of a letter from the Secretary of State to Mr. Baker. July 10, 1815. ASP FR 553.

"if they returned to Pensacola they would be slaves and here they were free." By April of 1815, another report described the occupants of the fort as determined to resist any effort to re-enslave them. "[They] say they will die to a man rather than return." That summer, additional reports described the military discipline being imposed at the fort where the "negros are saucy and insolent, and say they are all free."[23]

Even with the British and most of the Creeks and Seminoles gone, escapees from north of the border continued to seek out Negro Fort and the promise of freedom it held. As late as November 1815, Benjamin Hawkins reported that "An invitation has come up from the Seminoles to invite the negros in the Creek nation and frontiers of Georgia to come down and be free." Hawkins noted that "a considerable number of Negroes" arrived at Prospect Bluff that month fleeing plantation slavery.

To Andrew Jackson, hero of New Orleans, hater of the Spanish, self-made military genius, lawyer, land speculator, and erstwhile dealer in goods ranging from goose feathers to human slaves, the situation on the Apalachicola was intolerable. Jackson had became a national hero after leaving hundreds of Creek Indian skulls whitening on battlefields and in the charred ruins of Indian towns. His adulation by Americans was only heightened when, after crushing the British at the Battle of New Orleans, he sent the corpse of their commander back to London pickled in a barrel of rum. By 1816, Jackson set his sights on the oldest remnant of the ancient age of conquest—Spain's claim to Florida.

A series of letters exchanged between Jackson, his staff and U.S. officials chronicles what happened next in a tone of menace and doom:[24]

March 15, 1816
The Secretary of War to General Andrew Jackson
Sir, It appears from the representations of colonel Hawkins, that the Negro Fort, erected during

---

[23] Saunt,*A New Order of Things.* 282-285.
[24] "Letter from the Secretary of War, Transmitting, Pursuant to a Resolution of The House of Representatives, of the 26th Ult. Information in Relation to the Destruction of the Negro Fort, in East Florida, in the Month of July, 1816, &c. &c." Washington: E. De Krafft. 1819.

the war at the junction of the Chattahouchie and Flint Rivers, has been strengthened since that period, and now occupied by between two hundred and fifty and three hundred blacks, who are well armed, clothed and disciplined. Secret practices to inveigle Negroes from the frontiers of Georgia... are still continued by the Negroes and the hostile Creeks. This is a state of things which cannot fail to produce much injury to the neighboring settlements, and excite irritations which may ultimately endanger the peace of the nation.... Should it be determined, that the destruction of the fort does not require the sanction of the legislature, measures will be promptly taken for its reduction. From the representations of its strength, heavy cannon will be necessary to batter it...

March 20, 1816
General Edmund Gaines to Major General Andrew Jackson

...If intercourse could be opened down the Appalachicola, it would enable us to keep an eye upon the Seminoles, and the Negro Fort. The Negro establishment is (I think justly) considered as likely to produce much evil among the blacks of Georgia, and the eastern part of the Mississippi territory.

Will you permit me to break it up?

April 8, 1816
Maj. Gen. Andrew Jackson to Gen. Edmund Gaines

...If the conduct of these people is such as to encourage the Indian war; if the fort harbors the Negroes of our citizens ... or holds out inducements to the slaves of our citizens to desert from their owners' service, this fort must be destroyed... If they are stealing and enticing away our Negroes, they ought to be viewed as a band of out-laws, land pirates, and ought to be destroyed. Notify the gov-

ernor of Pensacola of your advance into his territory, and for the express purpose of destroying these
lawless banditti ... destroy it, and restore the stolen Negroes and property to their rightful owners.

Jackson condemned the Negro Fort as a "nest of banditti"
whose sole purpose was "murder, rapine and plunder." However, the
people in the Negro Fort who were characterized as murderous
bandits were anything but. In May of 1816, while the Americans
were making plans for the destruction of the Negro Fort, a merchant
with a trading company wrote to his superiors listing some of the
company's slaves who had fled to Prospect Bluff: "[T]he following
Negroes, who are now on the Bluff, the restoration of them appears
doubtful, to Wit—Billy & Lally & their children, Cressy, Flora, Beek,
Cynthia & Nero—Stephen & his wife Cynthia—Tom a House
servant."[25] Also at Negro Fort at Prospect Bluff were the Africa-born
escapees Congo Tom, Carlos Congo, and Carlos Mayumbe. The
Africans most highly valued as slaves at the Negro Fort were
Ambrosio, a shoemaker valued at 900 pesos, and Harry, a caulker
and navigator, who was valued at 2000 pesos because he knew how
to read and write.[26] Jackson's "nest of banditti" was made up of
sailors, master carpenters, coopers, ironsmiths, bakers,
laundresses, cooks, sawyers, masons and cartwrights—fathers,
mothers and children.

They were men, women and children seeking freedom, but
they were all bloody-handed murderers to Andrew Jackson. Although
the fort was located on sovereign Spanish soil, Jackson ordered the
"nest" to be wiped out. In April of 1816, Jackson did his diplomatic
due diligence and wrote to the new governor in Pensacola, Mauricio
de Zuniga, that if Spain didn't do something about the Negro Fort,
he would. Its continued presence would "compel us, in self-defense,
to destroy them." Jackson had no fear of provoking the Spanish with
his own invasion. He was just leaving a token paper trail to satisfy
potential critics in Washington. Jackson had learned from a spy in
Pensacola that the Spanish troops there had "not enough gunpowder
to fire a salute."[27]

---

[25] Edmund Doyle to R.C. Spencer. April 6, 1815. FHQ. Vol. 17. No. 3. Pp. 237-238.

[26] Landers, *Black Society in Spanish Florida*. 232.

[27] Report of Captain Amelung to General Jackson. June 4, 1816. ASP FR 557.

April 24, 1816
Maj. Gen. Andrew Jackson to the Secretary of War
....I have a hope that general Gaines has attended to the subject of this Negro Fort and put an end to the lawless depredations of this banditti of land-pirates. He has been left to his discretion to act on this subject, with my opinion, if certain facts can be proven against them, that their fort must be destroyed.

I trust he has taken the hint....

May 23, 1816
Gen. Edmund Gaines to Lt. Col. Duncan Clinch
I...have to direct that you will provide a boat, and dispatch it with an officer and fifty men, to meet the vessels from New Orleans, as soon as you are advised of their being on the river....Should the boat meet with opposition, at what is called the Negro Fort, arrangements will immediately be made for its destruction, and for that purpose, you will be supplied with two 18 pounders, and one howitzer...I have likewise ordered fifty thousand musket cartridges, some rifles, swords, etc. Should you be compelled against the Negro Fort, you will land at a convenient point above it, and force a communition with the commanding officer of the vessels below, and arrange with him your plan of attack....

June 15, 1816
Maj. Gen. Andrew Jackson to the Secretary of War
Sir, ...[T]here can be no fear of disturbing the good understanding that exists between us and Spain, by destroying their Negro Fort, restoring to, the owners the Negroes that may be captured.
The 4th and 7th infantry will be sufficient to destroy it....

During the next month, American troops and allied Creek Indians moved into position. The fighters at the fort beat back repeated land-based assaults by the Creeks under William McIntosh, forcing the Americans to call up gunboats to ascend the Apalachicola from the Gulf in order to shell the fort with artillery. On the morning of July 27, 1816, the gunboats opened fire on Negro Fort. After getting the range on the fort, one of the gunboats began to fire "hot shot," cannonballs heated red-hot in on-board furnaces. One of the shots landed in the powder magazine in the center of the fort, destroying the entire structure and most of its inhabitants in one massive explosion.

An American officer described the aftermath:

> You cannot conceive, nor I describe the horrors of the scene. In an instant, hundreds of lifeless bodies were stretched upon the plain, buried in sand and rubbish, or suspended from the tops of the surrounding pines. Here lay an innocent babe, there a helpless mother; on the one side a sturdy warrior, on the other a bleeding squaw. Piles of bodies, large heaps of sand, broken guns, accoutrements, etc. covered the site of the fort.[28]

There were approximately 50 survivors of the explosion, but most of those soon died of their wounds. Amazingly, Garson, the leader of the black forces, survived, but was quickly executed. The remaining survivors were returned to those who claimed to own them, and the wreckage of the fort was burned along with the bodies of the dead.

Five days later, Edmund Doyle, from the Forbes & Co. mercantile firm, was ascending the Apalachicola, directed by John Innerarity to go and retrieve the Africans that they claimed belonged to them. Doyle met the gunboats as they were returning to the Gulf. Doyle told them he was on his way to Prospect Bluff to round up the fugitive slaves that belonged to the company. The sailors on the gunboats told Doyle to turn around.

There was no one left alive at Negro Fort on Prospect Bluff.

---

[28] Army and Navy Chronicle. 2:115.

Spanish colonial black militia

Detail from "View of the town & castle of St. Augustine,"
1740 map depicting Oglethorpe's siege of St. Augustine.

Fort Gadsden explodes when an American shell hits the powder magazine, killing hundreds of former slaves and indian defenders. This is a reconstruction of U.S. gunboat response to an attack from British Fort (" Fort Nicholls" or "Negro Fort") and ensuing Powder Magazine Explosion, July 27, 1816. Painting by Pat Elliott of Negro Fort being shelled by the American army in 1816.

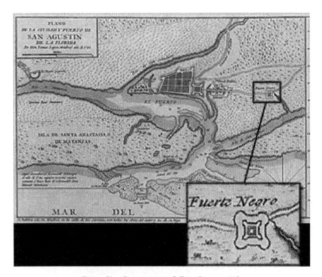

Detail of a map of St. Augustine
showing the position of Fort Mose ("Fuerte Negro")
on the outskirts of the city.

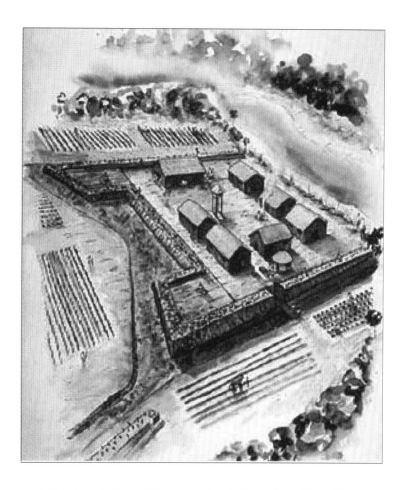

Artists' rendering of the reconstructed version of Fort Mose.

CHAPTER TWO

THE AFRICAN AMERICAN INSURGENCY*

1739-1858

Y. N. KLY**

Introduction

This presentation attempts to acquaint the reader with a war whose true nature has remained largely unacknowledged despite its decisive influence on U.S. historical development. It seeks to respond to the numerous questions that arise when one reviews existing data pertinent to the gamut of events, encounters, skirmishes, battles and wars that occurred in the South Carolina/Georgia/Florida region between 1739 (the Stono Rebellion) and 1858 (the ending of the "third Seminole War") in order to demonstrate that these events should be viewed as an important but seldom discussed war against slavery and colonization.

Occurring on an ongoing basis through uprisings, military skirmishes and battles which took place over the period of a century, the Gullah War[1] marked the resistance of enslaved Africans to the

---

'Due to the fact that at this early stage, the majority of the African Americans who fought this war still spoke the GUllah language and were defined as Gullahs or Geechees, earlier editions of this article referred to this African-American uprising as "The Gullah Wars".
**Assisted by Diana Kly.

[1] The term "Gullah Wars" was coined by Muriel Miller Branch in *The Water Brought Us*, Cobblehill Books/Dutton, New York, 1995, to refer to the ongoing and consistent Gullah resistance to enslavement, as manifested not simply in insurgency, but also in incendiary activities, poisonings, sabotage and flight. However, Ms. Branch did not further concern herself with the extensive insurgency surrounding the general flight of the Gullah to Florida, their establishment of communities there and normalized living patterns, their resistance to the state militia and later U.S. army incursions into what was then called Spanish-held Florida in order to destroy their communities and re-enslave them, and their subsequent removal and pursuit into Oklahoma and on into Mexico.
[2] We regard this prolonged conflict as a war composed of many battles, rather than as a series of wars, insofar as it evolved around a single major issue—the African resistance to enslavement and re-enslavement, and the threat that posed to the institution of slavery. In the course of this century-and-longer struggle, the issue was never fully resolved. The Gullah did not surrender,

institution of slavery in the U.S. colonies. For the length of its duration, this war[2] continued to pose a substantial threat to the successful maintenance and operation of the enslavement system, a threat acknowledged in historical writings,[3] historical data, and evident in the implacability with which, on the U.S. colonist and later federal side, it was pursued.

The fact that the true nature of a war occurring in the United States for over a period of a century has as yet to be fully acknowledged for what it was, suggests a socio-political manipulation of history that renders recovery possible only through a socio-political and historical analysis (Gabriel Almond). The socio-political reasons why the African American resistance to enslavement was largely unreported and unacknowledged during this historical period, was due to the threat that widespread knowledge of a largely successful (insofar as it was never fully quelled) African-American insurgency might have posed to the stability of a plantation system run on the labor of Africans, and thereby to the entire effort to enslave Africans in the U.S. colonies.

Whether acknowledgment of this war failed to surface in ensuing periods due to ongoing active suppression of information, the unquestioning acceptance of biased earlier documentation and the established parameters for viewing colonial history, or lack of courage, remains a topic for further research.

What we seek to do here is to break through the conceptual distortion to provide a clear understanding based on the acknowledged facts and sound historical analysis within the context of an unsual circumstance.

The African peoples brought to the U.S. to eventually be transformed into slaves for U.S. colonists came from various social sectors of numerous African nations. Some worked in colonists' homes and often interacted most frequently with Euro-Americans, thus assimilating a subordinate class form of Euro-American values and culture. For the masses who worked in the fields, however, this assimilation process was through indirect contact with the Euro-

---

and ultimately the institution of slavery, the issue which gave rise to this prolonged confrontation, was abolished due to exigencies related to the Civil War.

[3] The threat of this prolonged insurgency to the existence and maintenance of slavery is fully recognized in William Loren Katz, *Black Indians: A Hidden Heritage,* Atheneum Books, New York, 1986); Jan Carew, "The Undefeated: Joint Struggles of Native Americans and Peoples of the African Diaspora," in *Exploring the African American Experience,* edited by Niara Sudarkasa, Levi A. Nwachuku, Robert E. Millette and Judith A.W. Thomas, Cornell University Press, Ithaca, 1998; Kevin Mulroy, *Freedom on the Border: The Seminole Maroons in Florida, the Indian Territory, Coahuila, and Texas,* Texas Tech University Press, Lubbock, TX., 1993, among others.

Americans as well as a stronger assimilation among the various races of the Africans themselves. It would be the mission of those who were thought to be properly assimilated/educated (and placed in positions of leadership), to carry out the final stages of voluntary identification with the interests of the Anglo-American culture and politic, even if it meant the oppression of their own ethny or that of any other (while still not becoming equal-status Anglo-Americans themselves). For this same purpose, it would be important that they remained identified with the Africans.

The culture of Africans over time evolved into the ethnicity now known as African American, as happened with the Euro-Americans' stabilization into essentially an Anglo-American (popularly called, "white") culture. As more and more AFrican Americans were moved throughout the US and left their Gullah/Geechee culture, the remaining Gullah-Geechees began to be understood as a separate ethny. This type of orientation within the black community resulted in the creation of such bizarre entities as "black Indians,"[4] with great misconceptions about the Gullah and the history of the Gullah/Geechees.

The African role in what is popularly called the Seminole Wars[5] can most accurately be said to have begun around the time of the Stono Rebellion in South Carolina and the destruction of Negro Fort (see *The Broken Days*), and to have included the aborted Denmark Vesey revolt in Charleston, as well as other skirmishes and battles

---

[4] This is not to say, however, that as the subsequent resistance to cultural assimilation of those who successfully fled to Florida continued, it did not lead to their acquiring additional ethnic characteristics which may have distinguished them from what is generally regarded as African American culture at large.

[5] While the Seminole Wars could equally, and with justice, be called the American Anti-Slavery War, the African American/Euro-American War, the U.S./African War, etc., it would seem blatantly inadequate to refer to it as the Slave War any more than as the Seminole Indian War. The Africans and African Americans who fought these wars likely did not define themselves in terms of either their capture or enslavement. Referring to Africans as "slaves"—irrespective of whether or not they were even living under conditions of enslavement—was a U.S. colonist conceptualization fostered and enforced for socio-political reasons. The mass efforts to escape enslavement which they considered unjust and unacceptable serves as indisputable evidence that Africans and African Americans never accepted enslavement; they were more likely to have considered themselves to be captives. There is nothing in pre- or post-Civil War history to support this colonist conception of African Americans as slaves rather than enslaved except the fact that U.S. law and society so defined them. According to Porter, p. 33, "whites named those who escaped to Florida as 'Seminole Negroes' and had recognized them as an independent group during the Second Seminole War. We do not know how the maroons referred to themselves at this point."

which took place in South Carolina and what was called Florida. All these can be viewed as part of an ongoing resistance by captured Africans to the enslavement institutions. The anti-enslavement revolts and later military campaigns of the African "exiles" of Florida (like the Civil War) were undeniably of equal military significance.

As already noted, the original suppression of information was first and foremost an effort to keep the African American insurgency from becoming better known and more popular among other captured Africans and their potential allies among Indians and the indentured servants. Records of many of the more prominent military encounters indicate a predominant proportion of Africans.[6] The key battles were fought in Florida, a region whose militant population at the time was predominantly African and Indian.[7] As General Andrew Jackson wrote in 1818, the American motivation for the invasion of Florida was:

---

[6] Wild Cat's brother, a son of King Philip, was of African descent. Osceola's wife, Morning Dew, was of African descent. It may be that the marriage between "Morning Dew" and Osceola, plus his skills as a warrior, made it possible for Osceola to be projected as the leader of both the African American and Indian armies. It should be noted that Osceola was partially of European ancestry. As Celia Bland points out in *Osceola: Seminole Rebel,* "Osceola had not always been a Seminole, nor had he always lived in Florida." His great-grandfather was a Scottish hunter who settled with the Tallahassee Indians; the granddaughter of this marriage married an Englishman, and the son was named Billy Powell. In time, Billy Powell changed his name according to Creek custom, and became Asi Yaholo, or as the whites pronounced it, Osceola. (See Celia Bland, *Osceola: Seminole Rebel,* Chelsea House, New York, 1994, p. 21.) Indeed, dressed now in calico as had been prescribed by law in colonial settlements for Africans, now in a blue officer's jacket during the Battle of the Withlacoochee (Bland, *supra.,* p. 67), and surrounded by a Gullah bodyguard, one should be moved to speculate: just who was this man who had won such renown as an Indian warrior? As Bland further notes, "Osceola was often mistakenly identified as the chief of the Alachua Seminoles. This was Micanopy's position, one that the Tustenuggee Osceola could not have held, but at the time, whites often assumed that any Indian who spoke with authority in the councils or led warriors into battle was a chief. Osceola, as the nephew of Red Stick leader Peter McQueen, did hold an important position on Micanopy's council, and gained authority as a leader in battle. However, there is little doubt of the predilection of the colonial press for Osceola." (See Bland, *supra.,* p. 69). To what extent may this have been, even at this early time in history, yet another instance of the media deciding for itself who were the leaders of groups whose leadership processes or allegiances it did not, and did not care to, understand, or indeed, an instance of the predominating power deciding which among the contending leaders within an enemy group or nation, it preferred or refused to recognize?

[7] When General Jesup's troops stormed Osceola's headquarters in January 1837, fifty-two of the chief's fifty-five-man personal bodyguard were African (Katz, *supra.,* p. 60).

> To chastise a savage foe [the Spanish], who, combined with a lawless band of Negro brigands, have for some time past been carrying on *a* cruel and unprovoked war against the citizens of the United States...[8]

This plus the desire to colonialize the Indian lands provided the motivational forces for this war which spanned over a century: the implacable pursuit of U.S. colonists to enslave formerly captured Africans for motives which ranged from psychological (fury at the knowledge that those they felt were their inferiors could live in peace and socio-economic equality with other groups) to the desire to eliminate the threat that free communities of Africans posed to the continuation of the enslavement system.

The African American Wars

Wars are generally known and their major battles remembered by descendants of those who fought them, and this of course was true in relation to the African-American War. These battles started in South Carolina, in what were successful and unsuccessful anti-enslavement revolts—the unsuccessful revolts leading to the garden of death, and the successful ones to liberated Florida, the northern or western U.S., or Canada.[9] Due to the proximity of what was called Spanish Florida at the time, it was there that the masses of African Americans fled, allied with the First Nations peoples, and prepared to do battle.

After the fall of Negro Fort, almost continuous low-intensity conflict existed between the Africans and Indians, and the colonists.

---

[8] John K. Mahon, *History of the Second Seminole War, 1835-1842,* University of Florida Press, Gainesville, 1967, p. 26.

[9] Most historical accounts tend to separate and diminish the African American resistance, portraying it simply as flight either to the northern U.S., to Canada or to Florida. However, it seems more adequate to view all three of these actions as part of a generalized revolt *en masse* against enslavement which could be said to include the efforts of the abolitionists (including John Brown) as well as the flight leading to the Canadian settlements (particularly Africville in Halifax, etc.), as part of the Gullah War. John Brown has typically been discredited as having acted in almost lunatic isolation; however, were his actions to be viewed as occurring in the wake of a prolonged insurgency in Florida which sent its tremors through the entire coastal region, they might seem less out of context, albeit belated, since by the time of his death, the "third Seminole War" had already drawn to a close.

Historical records as well as the oral history traditions of the descendants of the African exiles in various parts of the Americas recall many of the major battles of this African-American War. An adequate elaboration of these battles and the convolution of events between and surrounding them would require more space than this article intends to admit. The following, however, is a general account of some of the most significant battles of this African-American War.

The Stono Rebellion, 1739

While we have decided to date the commencement of the African-American War at 1739, the date of the Stono Uprising, this is not to say that Gullah resistance had not been significant even before that time. Peter H. Woods notes:

> "[The Stono Uprising]... was preceded by a series of projected insurrections, any one of which could have assumed significant proportions. Taken together, all these incidents represent a brief but serious groundswell of resistance to slavery, which had diverse and lasting repercussions."[10]

A lengthy chapter in Woods' book, *Black Majority,* also deals with the subject of "Runaways" (self-liberated Africans). Woods provides numerous instances from historical records[11] of the unsuccessful efforts of enslaved Africans to escape, and indeed numerous details of records are provided indicating their recapture. The measures enacted to prevent the escape of captured Africans were so extensive and severe, and the records of *recapture* of fugitives so extensive, that one might well have wondered not only how any had managed to escape, but also how any had dared to try. While one might view the measures of control put in place by the colonists as so extensive as to have made flight and resistance near impossible, it is also possible to intuit by the very extent of the preventative measures,

---

[10] Peter H. Wood, *Black Majority: Negroes in Colonial South Carolina From 1670 through the Stono Rebellion,* Alfred A. Knopf, New York, 1974, pp. 308-309. Wood goes on to say that "The slave system in the British mainland colonies... never again faced a period of such serious unrest." However, if in fact the Gullah may be regarded as the major contenders and opponents in what have been called the "Seminole Wars," then clearly this is far from the case.

[11] Primarily marshals' reports, advertisements in newspapers, etc.

the extent of resistance and flight which must have either been happening, or at very least, been anticipated.

Eighteenth century Charleston newspapers ran ads for 2, 424 "runaways" [self-liberated Africans].[12] As noted by Murial Miller Branch, during this period, there were hundreds of "runaway African American *encampments*"[italics added] from the border of South Carolina to St. Augustine, Florida. Branch writes that "Approximately one hundred African Americans were killed or executed for their participation in the *Stono Rebellion*."[13] But for each African who was killed in an escape attempt, there was another rising up elsewhere to "escape."[14] Ms. Branch quotes a Sea Island *grio,* Janie Moore, as pointing out the location of the Stono rebellion and saying:

> This is where some Sea Island slaves began their rebellion back in 1739. They were trying to escape to Florida... The Stono Rebellion took place in St. Paul's Parish, near the western part of the Stono River. These rebels for freedom marched through South Carolina on their way to Spanish-held Florida, beating their drums, carrying a flag, and calling out "Liberty!" as they marched.[15]

---

[12] See William S. Pollitzer, "The Relationship of the Gullah-Speaking People of Coastal South Carolina and Georgia to Their African Ancestors", in Marquetta L. Goodwine et al., ed., The Legacy of Ibo Landing, Clarity Press, 1998.

[13] Ms. Branch, who seems to have confined her research efforts within the standard U.S. politico-historical framework, tells us much about the *failed* efforts of enslaved African Americans to escape to freedom in Spanish Florida, but little about the main event: the efforts and battles of those who succeeded in reaching Spanish Florida, and their successful launching of an anti-slavery war by encouraging other enslaved African Americans to escape, and by organizing militarily for self-defense, to protect themselves against recapture, barbaric torture, and re-enslavement. She mentions the "hundreds" of African American encampments only in passing. One might well presume that hundreds of encampments *en route* indicated a population of substantial numbers; these numbers should be added to those of the established villages and communities in Florida. Tyndell's Home Page (http://web.fie.com/~tonya/bblkindhtm) asserts that as early as the 1700s, there were over 100,000 "black Indians" [*sic*]. While these figures are usually contradicted by official U.S. statistics from this period, there is no particular reason to believe these statistics over information handed down from generation to generation.

[14] The fateful African (Ibo) mass suicide at Ibo Landing speaks for the African mood of that time, and is said to be the inspiration for the famous African American spiritual, "Oh, Freedom."

[15] The author quotes Janie Moore as going on to say that "None of the tours would ever have brought you out here just like they didn't take you by the Emmanuel A.M.E. Methodist Church where Denmark Vesey planned his uprising." Ms. Branch further states that "the site of the Stono Rebellion of 1739 is now the home of an

While this uprising was crushed, it evidenced what must have been a widespread awareness of the promise of freedom in Florida.

Battles with the state militia, 1736-1812

Assuredly, the enticement to flee to Spanish Florida existed.[16] According to Mulroy, "Runaways from South Carolina began arriving in St. Augustine as early as 1687." Likely this was because

> [t]he Spaniards welcomed runaways from southern plantations, gave them their freedom, and asked for little in return save for their cooperation in repelling elements hostile to both parties... In 1739, Montiano set aside for these fugitive Africans an armed garrison near St. Augustine called Gracia Real de Santa Teresa de Mose, which became the first known free black community in North America.[17]

A buffer zone protected by Gullah and First Nations warriors formed an integral part of Spanish defenses in Florida. This policy operated with some success. In 1812, faced with an invasion force from Georgia, "a force of Africans and Indians under black leadership cut the patriots' supply lines and finally raised the siege of St. Augustine."[18]

Mainstream historical writing typically portrays the Africans in Florida as escaped runaways who fled helter skelter through the bush to the security and protection offered by the "Seminole"[19] Indians

African American farm cooperative, but the memory of the rebellion is as fresh in Janie's mind as if she had actually been there to witness it."

[18] The Spanish, who still enslaved Africans and Indians by the hundreds of thousands in their colonial territories were, with an urbane cynicism, willing to offer freedom rather than to fight those captured by their imperial rivals, since these formerly-enslaved were staunch fighters who could protect a sparsely populated but strategically located colony. While policing the northern border of Spanish Florida, the armed African American militias, along with armed English, Indian, and African American farmers and cattle ranchers, were, in their own view, protecting their own interest. See Jan Carew, *supra.*

[17] Mulroy, *supra.,* pp. 8-9.

[18] Mulroy, *supra.,* p. 12.

[19] The word "seminole" is a Creek word meaning "runaway" or "exile." Though it later applied to both Indians and Africans, and even to Indians in Florida prior to 1814, the term came into existence after the defeat of the Creek Confederation in 1814 at the Battle of Horseshoe Bend, to apply to a section of the Creek who fled to

(who, prior to the defeat of the Creek Nation in 1814 were said to number some 2,000).[20] But African communities were already in existence in Florida at that time. And they were flourishing, due to African familiarity with a tropical climate, and knowledge of rice growing, for which the Africans were especially noted. In fact, as Joe Opala noted:

> From the beginning of Seminole colonization in Florida, the Indian may have depended upon African farmers for their survival.

This conjecture seems reasonable, since for that section of the Creek nation which had just fled into exile, the Florida terrain was substantially different from that of their own homelands. Here, Africans lived in well-built homes and raised fine crops of corn, sweet potatoes, vegetables and cotton. They owned herds of livestock, and hunted and fished. This is hardly the picture of disorganized, dependent and pitiable fugitives which arises from historical writings which consistently define the Africans in terms of their enslavement—either as slaves, runaway slaves, or maroons.

Florida. Those Creeks who refused to accept defeat, left their tribal lands, and fled to Florida, continued their struggle by joining with the Gullahs, who were also readily incorporated under the "exile" rubric expressed in the Creek word, "seminole." Those Creeks who remained were coerced into becoming subordinate to the U.S. colonist government. They were used to help fight the exiles (Seminoles) and to capture Africans and African Americans fleeing to Florida for the purposes of re-enslaving them. The U.S. colonists, for obvious socio-political reasons, preferred to use the Creek word for exile (seminole) to refer to all their anti-slavery adversaries in Florida, particularly the Gullah. Then, where it facilitated their interests, they attempted to identify this word only with the Indian exiles. See Joshua Giddings, *The Exiles of Florida,* University of Florida Press, Gainesville, 1964. The colonists, in their fanatical racist determination not to admit that Africans were capable of defending themselves, distorted the history of this war to such an extent that even African American and American Indian scholars today, who might otherwise find it difficult to conceptualize Africans as Indians, have not laid the distortion bare. We suggest that avenues for further study might include the democratic example of a fully developed multi-ethnic confederacy, as existed in Florida in the 18th and early 19th centuries (African, Indian, Spanish and English populations), and its possible example and influence upon subsequent efforts towards the establishment of multi-ethnic democracy. While today some 2,000 Seminole Indians live on 6 reservations in Florida, in the 1930s and '40s their attempts to organize for federal recognition purposes (pursuant to the Wheeler-Howard Act) were not successful, and did not succeed until 1957 when a majority of tribal members voted to establish the Seminole Tribe of Florida. Even then, a group among them seceded to become the Miccosukee Tribe in 1962. Further, the U.S. government has not seen fit to recognize those of African descent who termed themselves "Afro-Seminoles." (See Stacey Bomser and Janet Maizner, "History of the Seminole Tribe of Florida," Press Release, internet http: // www.seminoletribe.com/ news/access/ history.html.)

The liberated territory in Florida was populated by "a loose organization of associated towns enjoying a great deal of local autonomy and displaying a large measure of cultural diversity... The constituent members came from different regions and spoke various languages."[21] While most historical writing refers to the Africans in Florida as Seminoles,[22] the actual incorporation of Africans into the Confederacy was not as individuals who had been assimilated to an Indian culture, but rather as collective groups, living independently in their own communities and maintaining their own languages and ethnicity.

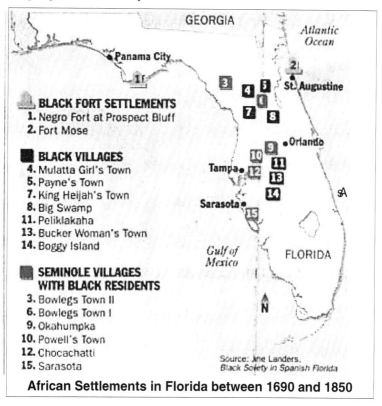

African Settlements in Florida between 1690 and 1850

[20] It swelled to 5,000 with the incursion of the Creek " runaways" in 1814. Cited in Katz, *supra.*, p. 50.

[21] Mulroy, *supra.*, p. 7. Mulroy refers to this as the "Seminole Confederation."

[22] Whether black Seminoles, Seminole Negroes, Seminole maroons. See Mulroy, *supra.*, p. 1. Mulroy notes "This term, Seminole Negroes, would become prominent in the writings of white observers during the mid-to-late 1830s and contribute to outside perceptions that the maroons constituted a separate group." p. 18. Mulroy goes on to note: "By that time, the group clearly had self perceptions as a corporate body, also." But as Seminoles? It is reasonable to assume that such an identification would come later?

As Mulroy noted, "The black towns fitted easily into the confederation but, with few exceptions, the Indians did not consider Africans to be Seminoles"[23]— if "seminole" were construed to mean "Indian" as opposed to "runaway" or "exile." Presumably, neither did the Africans consider themselves to be Seminoles, i.e. assimilated to Indian culture.

> While certain aspects of the maroons' and Seminoles' daily lives were similar, others were not. The differences formed the bases of the maroons' ethnicity and defined them as a people...The maroons' first language was what linguist Ian F. Hancock has termed Afro-Seminole, a creole related to Gullah... The [Indian] Seminoles' native tongue remained either Hitchiti or Muskogee.[24]

Similar to the situation in Haiti,[25] the political and military circumstances created by the efforts of three European governments––England, France and Spain—to claim the same area of the Americas in confrontation with the emerging revolutionary American nation facilitated the African and First Nations[25] efforts to secure weapons to pursue their own best interests. They sought freedom from captivity and the end of colonialism. They created (in effect) a multi-racial egalitarian democracy.[26] The European strategy of so-called "freeing

---

[23] Mulroy, *supra.,* p. 21.

[24] Mulroy, *supra.,* p. 22.

[25] As in the contest between the Spanish, English and French for control of Haiti, the contending European states, not having sufficient population on the land, chose the strategy of arming the Africans (assuring that they would fight for their freedom from whomever was enslaving them) and relying on them to withstand or overthrow the particular European power in place. There is little indication that any of these powers were less against African enslavement than the U.S. colonists — indeed, the Spanish and English participated in the slave trade at that time, themselves. However, they were willing to give support to the African American anti-enslavement effort, if it offered the only possibility of holding on to their American colonial possessions or securing new ones.

[25] The term "First Nations" is used here to describe the American Indians who allied with the Gullah. While typically employed in Canada rather than in the U.S. as yet, this term seeks to recognize the Indian peoples as nations, while indicating their aboriginal rights. It is particularly useful to describe those Indians who allied with the Gullah, since they likely consisted of a number of Indian nations such as the Yuchi, Hitchiti and Alabamas, insofar as, at that time, there was no such thing as a Seminole Indian tribe or nation in the ethnic sense, and the word seminole itself meant "runaway" or-"exile."

[26] Indeed, viewing the relations between Seminole Indians and the African communities in Florida prior to its acquisiton by the U.S. in 1819, one might even say

the slaves" so that they would fight against those who had captured them, which would leave the Africans totally at the mercy of the European countries which assisted them.

Motivation for Alliance

a) The Spanish supplied arms and political recognition to the Africans so that they might protect the political border between Spanish Florida and South Carolina.[28] These borders were constantly threatened by aggression from the American colonists in South Carolina.

b) The English also supplied Africans with some arms, military fortifications, and safe passage to Canada. They hoped to spur African and Indian resistance to the U.S. breakaway, revolution and permanent settlement. Many in England wished to discourage the U.S. colonists from First Nations land grabs and slavr labor as credible incentives for seeking independence from England.[29] They also sought to curtail these practices through limiting colonial expansion in the west, and disallowing slaveholding in Georgia.

c) A significant number of formerly-indentured servants sought personal freedom and economic opportunity by joining the African and their allies in the liberated territories.[30]

d) Last and most important (next to Spanish and English supply of arms and political space) was the African alliance with the First Nations.[31] This was by far the most natural and strategic alliance,

---

that this multi-racial democracy was practiced with the inclusion of a concept of minority rights; the Africans lived in autonomy in their own villages, and participated as equals in military campaigns, etc., contributing only a minor portion of their produce to the other group, whose own internal relations were collectivist. The difference between U.S. colonists' notions of "ownership" and those of the Indians was so extensive that one might properly question whether using this term in relation to Seminole Indian "ownership" of Africans was in any way appropriate, given its connotations for English-speaking peoples. On the other hand, its propaganda effect (maintaining the notion of Africans as people who could not be seen otherwise than as being owned by somebody) is indisputable.

[28] It was a force of Africans and Indians under black leadership which cut the patriots' supply lines and finally raised the U.S. siege of St. Augustine. See Mulroy, *supra.,* p. 12.

[29] In 1814, Lord Cochrane issued a proclamation which invited enslaved Africans to board his vessels along with their families, providing them with the option either to serve in His Majesty's navy or settle as free persons in the British West Indies. Such a proclamation was not based on humanitarian intervention, however, for slavery was still widespread elsewhere in the British empire.

[30] One finds in the early colonial slave codes repeated mention of "Negro and other enslaved." See Giddings, *supra.,* p. 2. The "other" were the Native Americans and some whites. Also see Buckmaster, *supra,* p. 29.

[31] The epic struggle waged by the African and Indian exiles (seminoles) in Florida between 1739 and 1858 can be viewed as a continuation of one that had begun in the

providing both logistics and manpower. The First Nations were interested in preventing the European settlers from usurping the land, whose usage they considered their right. They likely saw the Africans as posing no threat to their way of life—not only because the Africans were not attempting to impose their culture or way of life, or take possession of the right to determine land usage, but equally because the Africans were in no position to do so. In the most true sense, both were exiles: the captive Africans exiled from their home in Africa, and the First Nations from their tribal lands in America.[32] It seems likely that the Africans may have represented themselves to the First Nations as persons ultimately wanting to be free to return to their homelands in Africa. The religious beliefs of many of these African Americans indicate that the worst thing that could happen to them after death was for their spirit not to find its way home to their families, and therefore be left to wander endlessly.[33]

The negative aspect of the African alliance with the Indian First Nations was that it provided the U.S. colonists with a credible cover to disguise the fact that Africans were resisting their captivity "en masse," and posing a credible politico-military threat to the existence of the colonies, and thereby to the American revolution itself.[34]

It can safely be presumed that the colonial leadership's real politik would seek to prevent those Africans who remained captive from knowing about what was occurring nearby. The fear of another Haiti

---

first four decades of the Colombian era when Africans and Native Americans had joined forces against the Spanish colonizers in Hispaniola and Puerto Rico. See Jan Carew, *supra.* Such united struggles of Africans and Native Americans were to continue in the Americas in the decades and centuries afterwards. "They were," as Patterson explains with respect to the cimarron communities, "the dialectical response, the desires and struggles, of the multitudes who did most of the real work in the Indies to improve the quality of their lives." Thus such black and Indian alliances are known to have existed in southern Mexico, Central America, the Caribbean, the Guianas, the Brazilian northeast, and North America throughout the colonial period and beyond.

[32] Similar to succeeding generations of scholars referencing his work, Giddings, in *The Exiles of Florida,* refers to African American escapees from the Carolinas to Spanish-owned Florida by various labels—fugitive slaves, fugitive Negroes, Negro Indians, Seminoles, and exiles—but it should be emphasized that Giddings referred to "exiles" as the most appropriate because the captured Africans were uprooted from their own homeland and permanently exiled in the Americas, while colonialism and conquest made the Native Americans exiles in their own land.

[33] Georgia Workshop Project, *Drums and Shadows,* University of Georgia Press, 1945.

[34] The constant escape of the enslaved—African, Creek, and a small number of whites—was the principal reason for Spain's "establishing a free colony between South Carolina and Florida... it was thought that this colony being free (sic) would afford the planters of Carolina no protection against the future escape of [those they considered to be] their slaves from their service." Giddings, *supra,* p. 3.

was forever on the minds of the colonists.[35] The colonists would portray the Indians to the captured Africans as people who would either enslave them or help recapture them if they escaped.

There was a need to hide this insurgency not only from the captive Africans themselves, but also from world public opinion at large. The maintenance of the illusion that captured Africans were content with their situation and that the American revolution was for democracy, human rights, freedom, etc. served to encourage European immigration into Carolina, and to prevent panic and out-migration by those already there. It assured settlers and potential immigrants from Europe that all was going well and according to plan, and that the only wars involved the Indians. Such wars were already well known to the world.

By creating new Indian tribes on paper, accrediting as leaders only those Indians who would cooperate with them, and inciting individuals from existing Indian tribes to capture Africans, the early colonists were able to turn the Indian nations against each other, and neutralize the natural affinity between the struggle of African Americans for freedom, and that of the Indian First Nations for the end of colonialism. This U.S. legacy of divide and rule can be observed today in the tendency of the U.S. government to attempt to divide African Americans from any African, Asian, or European nation that recognizes and expresses the natural affinity between its struggle against the global political and socio-economic hegemony of the U.S.and the African American struggle for human rights.[36]

A few observations from early historical writings to more contemporary scholarship may alert future researchers to beware of the tendency of states to rewrite history in the terms of the political victors.

a) When reports from the battlefield involved the Africans, the words "black," "Negro" or "African" were simply omitted, or replaced by asterisks. This served to prevent the African American community from knowing that the Africans were in the process of conducting a successful insurrection. It was itself a tactic in the colonist war against that insurrection. It also prevented records of the African

---

[35] Prior to the successful U.S. revolution of 1776, and the conquest of Spanish Florida, the colonists also had an interest in keeping their enslaved African populations from knowing of the (self-)interest of the English and Spanish powers in assisting the cause of the enslaved, thereby forestalling any notion of outside help or alliances.
[36] The main ploy of the newly independent U.S. was the ancient Roman one of divide and conquer.

nature of this war from being picked up by later more fair-minded scholars (black, white or Indian) when they researched these earlier texts and newspapers for historical data.[37] It also succeeded in bedazzling the later researchers and scholars with confusing data, thus distorting their conceptualization of what had actually occurred.

b) Reports from the battlefield were frequently not even released to the public until a later date. For instance, the *South Carolina Gazette* had refrained from even mentioning the early Stono Uprising, which had occurred within a scant twenty miles of Charleston,[38] and

---

[37] As before mentioned, the reason for suppressing knowledge about this war at the time as well as during the later period of segregation (which extended until the 1960's) should be relatively easy to understand from a purely socio-political perspective. However, what is more difficult to comprehend is how the suppression of information to African American and Indian scholars was managed, particularly during the period of segregation when African American public education was under the direct management of African American colleges and high schools. These factors, coupled with the call for U.S. patriotism and assimilation into the dominant American ethny as a means of achieving equality, wealth, respect, etc. left little room or inclination for scholars to dig below the surface to uncover the true story of what came to be popularly or expediently known as the *"Seminole* Wars."

[38] According to Giddings *(supra.,* p. 29-30), records of the real objective of the earliest battles of the war—to recapture exiled African Americans—were disguised. Giddings writes: "Under the command of the Adjutant-General, another army crossed the border into Florida with the avowed intent of exterminating the "seminoles;" the real object was the recapture and the re-enslavement of the African American refugees... But when (that army) re-emerged from the rank, brutal thickets of Northern Florida, all military glory had been left behind. Wild men, they said, had sprung at them from every bush, cut off their supplies, decimated their men and bloodied their uniforms... One interesting detail emerged for the first time: African American 'soldiers' were mentioned by the Georgians and the Carolinians. Mentioned in passing, it is true, and their skill deprecated—and all mention deleted from the newspaper accounts. But however many asterisks the editors of the *Savanna and Charleston* (newspapers) inserted in the reports (informing their readers that the deletions were for reasons of local security), an incontestable fact had been established: that African Americans, organized in bands, well armed, had successfully fought a regiment of American soldiers... A second army was raised and went to seize eastern Florida and wipe out the African American settlements. It took the [so-called] slave-owners two years to grasp the fact that this army was also defeated. They sent in more men with guns. The African Americans and Indians, who were masters at fading into the dense swamps and forests, lost a few men and some cattle but claimed that not a single African American was captured... Some of the Georgians brought back tales of extraordinary courage, of African Americans and their Indian allies fighting together, the Indians under the leadership of Indians, the African Americans under the leadership of African Americans—and the great devotion between the two groups." (Giddings, *supra.,* p. 29).

was subsequently regarded as a major uprising in the state. The U.S. public heard nothing about the destruction of Negro Fort, which occurred in 1816, until 1837, when Congressman William Jay broke the story.[39] When General Gaines moved his troops out to burn down the African town of Fowltown, "believing it was best for citizens to learn little of the mounting U.S. war in Florida, the U.S. Secretary of War kept Congress in the dark."[40] This was typical of the practice of nonrecognition of African insurgency.[41]

c) When referred to specifically, the Africans were frequently mentioned in such a way as to minimize and denigrate African participation. For instance, in 1822, the U.S. Secretary of State reported that in Florida there were "five or six hundred maroon negroes wild in the woods."[42] This became a typical image of "maroons": terrified fugitives crashing through the bush, disorganized and isolated from each other, rather than free Africans functioning effectively as guerrilla units or living in communities.

If Africans who had successfully fled were mentioned, they were mentioned so that the nomenclature itself differentiated them from the bulk of the African population who still were captured. They were then referred to as Seminoles (a term without apparent African content), or as Seminole Negroes, Black Seminoles, Seminole maroons, etc.

Any mention of joint Seminole Indian and African American initiatives always put the Africansh in the "Tonto" position: "the Seminoles and their allies," "the Seminoles and the blacks," etc. African presence in peace negotiations was always accounted for by their appearing as "interpreters," etc., rather than as leaders or persons whose assent to agreements was required.

Perhaps to English-speaking readers and writers this seemed only natural, since, as far as they were concerned, the Africans were "owned" by the Seminole Indians in the way that the English understood ownership.

d) By referring to this insurgency which the militias were unable to quell as a "Seminole" insurgency, reports disguised the nature of the population against whom they were fighting.[44] As Mulroy

---

[39] Wood, *supra,* p. 298.

[40] Katz, *supra.,* p. 55.

[41] *ibid.*

[42] Indeed, this might be said to be typical of American reportage of the African American struggle in general—or of reportage of any contemporary entity, as it concerns the efforts and perspectives of those whom it seeks to suppress.

[43] Katz, *supra.,* p. 57.

[44] As Henrietta Buckmaster stated in her book, *The Seminole Wars:* "From now on, whenever 'Seminole' is referred to, it will mean Indian and Negro together. American policy linked them. The effort, then and later, to stress the "Indian"

acknowledges, "In what turned out to be a taste of things to come, moreover, it was the blacks who did most of the fighting in what is considered to be the main battle of the First Seminole War."[45] As far as the second Seminole War is concerned, General Jesup noted in December, 1836, "This, you may be assured, is a negro and not an Indian war."[46]

e) Ignoring the existence of African leaders further disguised the Gullah insurgence. While the name of Osceola has been justly celebrated, it should be remembered that he perished at the age of 34 in Fort Moultrie, years before the end of the Seminole Wars, and that only months before, he had been surrounded by a personal bodyguard in which Africans numbered 52 out of a total of 55.[47] John Horse, Ibrahim(or Abraham)[48] and Billy Bowlegs numbered among the foremost leaders of what have historically been referred to as the Second and Third Seminole Wars. Perhaps the colonists were more willing to recognize Osceola as their adversary, particularly given the degree of his European ancestry.[49]

Indeed, while Ibrahim went to meet with U.S. president, John Quincy Adams, at the negotiating tables in Washington, and John Horse later went to meet with President Polk, the significance of

---

nature of the conflict and ignore the African American was a part of that curious myopia which had denied to the Negro American the forthright part he took in his own destiny." (See Henrietta Buckmaster, *supra.*, p. 42). However, what might be dismissed as "curious myopia" should rather be viewed as intentional and strategic misinformation which attempted to deny an existing insurgency then and later, in order to forestall a widening of the insurgents' ranks. A similar strategy is seen today in the consistency of U.S. governmental policy and news media efforts to cast the total African American struggle for development within the context of the search for assimilation and civil rights, while ignoring (as much as possible) other equally important leadership directions.

[45] Mulroy, *supra.*, p. 16.

[46] Katz, *supra.*, p. 60. Jesup also noted: "Throughout my operations I found the negroes the most active and determined warriors, and during the conferences with the Indian chief I ascertained that they exercised an almost controlling influence over them." Seminole agent Thompson expressed his belief that "one of the major causes of Seminole hostility to removal was 'the influence which it is said the negroes, the very slaves in the nation, have over the Indians.'" No matter what the facts indicated the situation to be, for Thompson, the negro could only be a slave.

[47] Mulroy, *supra,* p. 28.

[48] While most accounts refer to this Gullah leader as Abraham, it is highly possibly that the name he called himself, *i.e.* his own name, was Ibrahim, a Muslim name, which then was mispronounced, intentionally or not, by the colonists, who were more likely to recognize the name as Abraham or to "correct" it to Abraham. Pictures of Ibrahim or Abraham show him wearing what appears to be an Islamic head dress. See following page.

[49] See Endnote 5.

their presence has been routinely disguised by referring to them as 'interpreters' for the Indians, rather than as leaders in their own right. The recognition of the African leadership would have had a profound effect in relation to the institution of slavery, and its political impact on the masses of captive Africans still yearning to be free.

The Treaty of Multrie Creek, signed in 1824, conceded a reservation of 4 million acres plus a yearly annuity, farming implements, a school, a blacksmith, and a gunsmith in exchange for the so-called Seminole Indians' forbidding so-called runaway slaves from their reservation. Not only did these Indians continue to abet fugitive Africans; they even demanded that the so-called slave catchers return the free Africans they had kidnapped from their villages.[50] Even in 1837, when the Seminoles were forced to sign a treaty accepting to no longer harbor "their negroes, their bona fide property," they ignored it.[51]

The U.S. sought to inculcate a mutual antipathy between Africans and Indians by keeping the African American and Indian peoples in general ignorance (insofar as was possible) concerning their alliance in resistance, by engendering situations and conceptualizations that encouraged anti-African propaganda to Indians, and anti-Indian propaganda to African Americans. It is little wonder that some among the Indians gave in to the U.S. government's temptations.[52] Even today, some African Americans and Indians prefer to view

---

[50] Bland, *supra.,* p. 44.

[51] At first, the treaty had provided that the Indians would relocate to the Indian Territories in the west "secure in their lives and property... [and] their negroes, their bona fide property *[sic]*, shall accompany them," but this so enraged the Florida slave hunters that this provision had had to be rescinded. As Bland noted, "Allowing so many runaways to migrate west [i.e. allowing so many self-liberated Africans to remain free] threatened the very institution of slavery." (See Bland, *supra.,* p. 89.)

[52] As a result of the retreat of the main forces of the alliance under African American leadership into Mexico to avoid defeat, capture, and re-enslavement or execution, some First Nations former allies of the Gullah found it expedient, with the assistance of the U.S. Bureau of Indian Affairs, to consolidate their interests and identity under the entity known as the Seminole Indian Tribe which exists today. However, this same hidden history has led to somewhat contradictory uncontested claims by blacks (formerly Gullah) who find it expedient to call themselves the Afro-Seminoles—"Afro" because the U.S. government, like its predecessors, continues to find it politically expedient to officially recognize only Indians as Seminoles. It was stated by one Gullah historian who investigated this Afro-Seminole group that they still speak "old" Gullah. Notes from conversation in Montreal with Marquetta L. Goodwine, Director of the Gullah/Geechee Sea Island Coalition, December, 1997. This Coalition was founded in 1996, and is concerned with soliciting support for Gullah survival. This "old Gullah" itself has been referred to as "the language they call Seminole." (See Art Chapman,

Seminoles as Indians who enslaved the Africans instead of as an Indian African alliance. This preference might well reflect a natural societal desire to be identified upward with the victorious, rather than downward with the African minority.

All of the encounters through 1812-13 were relatively small compared with the battles to come.

During most of this period, the U.S. colonists, bred on notions of African inferiority, seemed convinced that the Africans and their allies could pose no real threat to their colonialist and enslavement systems. They preferred to project the notion that they would be able to capture and eventually enslave the Africans. However, after state militia expeditions into Georgia met with numerous defeats, they began to change their minds.

In the years 1812 and 1813, African defenders figured largely in blocking the efforts of the Georgia "Patriots" to conquer the Georgia portion of what was called Spanish Florida. Militarily speaking, the Patriots faced hit and run skirmishes in which neither side achieved victories on the battlefield, and during which most of the losses were suffered by the militias. From the point of view of the militias' objectives of capturing Africans, these expeditions were a complete failure. Thus they served to convince the U.S. colonists that state militias would be unable to provide the force necessary to stop the African American insurrection.

At this stage, the colonists called for the assistance of the continental U.S. army. The enforcement of their colonialist and enslavement system would have to face trained and armed Africans under relatively equal military conditions. They experienced great shock at not being able to outmaneuver or outflank them.

These military failures shook their racist assumptions of moral and intellectual superiority. To restore the personal faith of their soldiers in the stability of the socio-political system and to prevent the settler population from wanting to abandon slavery (or more particularly, the struggle to preserve it)—thereby forsaking its economic advantages which had numbered among the reasons for colonizing America in the first place—the U.S. colonists needed to overcome the insurgency or at least disguise the true nature of whom they were fighting against.

After all, the collapse of the enslavement system in Haiti led to the collapse of French efforts to settle it, and likewise their problems may have dimmed their interest in settlement of the Louisiana territories as well. After all, without African slave labor, the Golden Triangle would turn to brass.

"Black Seminole Indians: Descendants honor heroes history almost forgot," *Star-Telegram,* September 22, 1997.

Then came a period of great uncertainty for the colonists, both North and South. The African insurgency raised the more disturbing question of whether the colonialist and enslavement system could be continued without the almost certain eventuality that the South would become African and Indian, and hostile. The only way that this apprehension could be put to rest without establishing an egalitarian multi-racial democracy would be to utterly destroy or devastate the African-Indian alliance and to obliterate their existence from historical memory.

The Battle at Horseshoe Bend, 1814

In 1814, General Andrew Jackson crushed the combined forces of the Creek Confederation at Horseshoe Bend on the Tallapoosa River. By imposing a treaty upon the defeated Creek Confederation which ceded several million acres to the Americans in such a way that it sundered and fragmented the Creek lands, Jackson made it impossible for them to exist any longer as a cohesive society. The Creek divided in two: those who submitted to the U.S. colonists' agenda, and those who resisted. Some five thousand warriors and their families (the exiles) followed the indomitable Creek leader, Sacafoca, over the border into Florida to ally with the African forces and other allied First Nations groups.[53] The defeat of the Creek Confederation and the movement of Chief Sacafoca into alliance with the African freedom fighters provided the extra manpower for what can be called the grand alliance of the "exiles" against the U.S. continental army.

The Battle of Negro Fort, 1816

The second Anglo-American war was marked by British efforts to ally with both Indians and escaped Africans. To that end, two British sloops of war and some smaller vessels landed troops in Appalachicola Bay under Lieutenant-Colonel Edward Nichols. He provided a large force of First Nations and African American insurgents with arms and ammunition. He proceeded to build a fort on the east side of the Appalachicola river, some thirty miles from its mouth, which was then taken over by the African American insurgents to serve as a bulwark against aggressions by the colonists. It became known by the U.S. colonists as *"Negro Fort,"* and by many captured Africans as the place to flee to for safety from enslavement.

---

[53] Carew, *supra,* includes among them the Tallahassees, the Muskhogeans, and the Mikasukis. Note Mulroy, *supra.,* indicated that the Creek exiles raised the Seminole population to 5,000, not increased it by this amount.

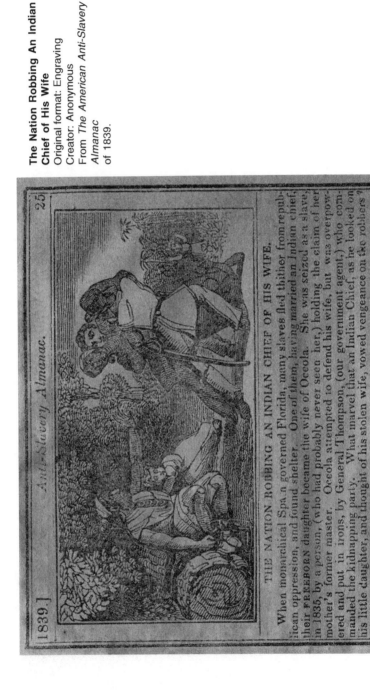

[1839.]   *Anti-Slavery Almanac.*   25

THE NATION ROBBING AN INDIAN CHIEF OF HIS WIFE.

When monarchical Spain governed Florida, many slaves fled thither from republican oppression, and found shelter. One of them, having married an Indian chief, their FREEBORN daughter became the wife of Oceola. She was seized as a slave, in 1835, by a person, (who had probably never seen her,) holding the claim of her mother's former master. Oceola attempted to defend his wife, but was overpowered and put in irons, by General Thompson, (our government agent,) who commanded the kidnapping party. What marvel that, an Indian Chief, as he looked on his little daughter, and thought of his stolen wife, vowed vengeance on the robbers?

Abraham

Osceola, mid-19th century engraving.

Coacoochee, or Wildcat

67

With a force of some three hundred men, women and children (of which 35 were Indians)[54] directed by black officers under the leadership of Commander Garcon,[55] it served as one of the most strategic African American fortifications.

Due to the cooperation of their Creek allies, the U.S. army had been unable to reach it by land. However, after crushing the Creek confederation at the Battle of Horseshoe Bend and meeting with unyielding African resistance on the land route to Negro Fort, the new U.S. government released the combined sea and land forces of the continental army to deter the African component of the war. U.S. naval and land forces invaded Spanish territory without a formal declaration of war, and destroyed Negro Fort in July, 1816, two years after it was built.

> Each side fired off cannonballs that landed harmlessly in the mud or shallow water. Eight times U.S. ships fired and eight times no one inside Fort Negro was hit. A ninth cannonball, heated red hot in a ship's furnace, landed with miraculous accuracy inside the fort's ammunition dump.[56]

Giddings describes what ensued:

> [A] blazing hell followed. The agonizing screams could be heard above the crescendo of explosions... That holocaust killed one-third[57] of those [African Americans] who had fled to Florida for safety. The Indians who died with them had been their friends and families... By Jackson's orders, any 'leaders' were to be handed over to [their defeated] Creeks[58] for torture. The sixty-two injured [those who survived] were carted away... [and enslaved] by

---

[54] Katz, *supra.*, p. 54.
[55] The uncertainty which surrounds much of the research concerning the Seminole is indicated by the fact that three of the major writers on the subject (Katz, Porter, Mulroy) are unable to agree on the name of the man who was commander of Fort Negro, site of one of the more celebrated battles of the first Seminole War.
[56] Katz, *supra.*, p. 55.
[57] This figure appears questionable, since it would place the number of Gullah in Florida as less than 1,000.
[58] Creeks who had submitted to the U.S. government upon the collapse of the Creek Confederation.

Drawing of a chickee and
lithograph of a Gullah Seminole town circa 1835.

anyone who claimed them—and they need offer no proof.[59]

The destruction of Negro Fort marked a turning point in the strategy of the African American leadership. Henceforth, they would avoid fighting from fixed, fortified positions, and return to their traditional guerrilla-oriented tactics. They would strike and vanish, maintain many hidden arms caches, lure the enemy into the swamps, forests and pastures where they enjoyed the advantage of knowledge of the land, and live constantly in a state of preparedness of the whole community for flight.

The Battle of Suwanee, 1818

In 1972, Northwestern University Professor Emeritus Jan Carew interviewed an aged descendant of the African American insurgents, an African American migrant to Andros Island in the Bahamas, and was given an account of the Battle of Suwanee in 1818:

> I heard 'bout the battle of Swanee' against Stonewall Jackson, my grandmother tell me 'bout it and her grand-mother tell her 'bout it long before. Stories like that does come down to us with voices in the wind. She tell me how the Old Ones used to talk 'bout the look on them white soldiers' faces when they see Black fighters looking like they grow outta the swamp grass and the hammocks, coming at them with gun and cutlass. Jackson get hurt at Swanee, man, the ancestors brutalize him there. He run away, and never come back to face Blacks and Seminoles fighting shoulder-to-shoulder—black flesh touching red and brown—that kind of thing does give the white man nightmare and day-fever all at the same time. But after them Black and Seminole fighters punish Jackson good and proper, he turn on the women and children that the Seminoles did leave behind, and any of them that look like they had African blood, he carry off to sell into slavery. Oh, God! That man Jackson was cruel, eh! *He enslaved them who was free already for two and three generation. He sell the grandchildren of former enslaved to the grandchildren of former slave owners!* [Italics added.] My old face already beat against eighty-odd-years and my children and grandchildren all gone to far places looking for work and a better life. But when Jesus of Nazareth decide to

---

[59] Mulroy, *supra*, p. 29

send Mantop to carry me to the Great Beyond, wherever my blood-seed scatter, they will spread the word 'bout how Black and Seminole ancestors fights side by side at Swanee.[60]

As Jan Carew noted, the old woman had been talking about the Battle of Suwanee, claimed by General Andrew Jackson as a victory, despite his troops having failed to defeat a heavily outnumbered force of African and First Nations insurgents who disappeared in the swamps and bayous after having inflicted heavy casualties on their attackers. The only victory he achieved was over a settlement of women and children who were noncombatants residing in their villages.[61] In Carew's own words:

> Looking at that old woman with hair like combed and bleached Sea Island Cotton, an age-serrated, benign ebony face and a white clay pipe held between teeth grooved by an infinite number of pipe stems, I almost considered it a miracle that, after more than a decade of following promising leads that had often turned out to be useless, I should have, quite unexpectedly, stumbled upon her eloquent testimony. There she was, telling me quite calmly between puffs on her clay pipe about a battle that Joshua Giddings described as 'the bloody Seminole war of 1816-1818, (which) arose from the efforts of... the U.S. Government to sustain the interests of slavery.'[62] This 1816-18 war to re-enslave those who had liberated themselves from slavery and to conquer Native American territory, is officially known as the 'First Seminole War.' This grandmother... was in fact telling me about an event that had taken place a century and a half earlier, and she was doing this on the island of Andros, one of the farthest outposts to which descendants of [liberated African Americans and their Indian allies] had escaped after the war had ended in the 1850s.[63]

However inadequately achieved Jackson's purported victory

---

[60] Carew, *supra*.
[61] *ibid.*
[62] Giddings, *supra*, p. 15
[63] Carew, *supra*.

at Suwanee might have been, he went on to smash through the African towns under the leadership of Billy Bowlegs. By May 24, he had captured Pensacola, and Florida fell into U.S. hands.

At this point, in confrontation with the U.S. army and no longer enjoying the political protection and arms provided by Spain[64] or England,[65] the African/ First Nations alliance lost the strategic assets which once might have allowed it the hope of withstanding assault by the U.S. indefinitely. The U.S. army pursued the exiles into southern Florida, undertaking with them, there, a series of negotiations and enticements in hope of terminating the effective alliance between the two enemy forces. In particular, the U.S. sought to promote the practice of slaveholding among the Africans' Indian allies.

After 1819, the central focus of U.S. policy in Florida would be to re-enslave the captive Africans who had liberated themselves, and, by trickery and further treaty, to expel the Indian First Nations from lands given to them by treaty in Florida.

Realizing that defeat meant re-enslavement, the African Americans played a decisive role in fostering and strengthening the exile alliance's opposition to removal, an opposition which unquestionably paved the way for the onset of what is known as the Second Seminole War.[66]

The Denmark Vesey Conspiracy, 1822

Despite the efforts of the U.S. to prevent knowledge of the African insurgency in Florida, it appears highly unlikely that this would have been completely successful. In the course of the implacable pursuit of the Africans by the U.S., many were captured (either through the efforts of colonists, or their Indian and African American allies who joined the Christian religion, and returned to captivity. However, the subsequent dispersal of ex-warriors throughout the slaveholding territories was likely to have proliferated word of African battles with U.S. colonists, and with the U.S. military.[67] This, combined

---

[64] As a result of the Peninsular Wars against Napoleon and the slaughter of Spanish subjects in Florida, Spain sold Florida (which was divided between Georgia and present day Florida) to the United States for five million dollars. While Spain attempted to prolong its protection through clauses in the treaty which stated that those in the territory who were free should remain so, this feeble attempt was soon disregarded. At this point, the victory of the insurgents became militarily impossible.

[65] Having by this time accepted its defeat in the American revolutionary war, Britain's natural strategic alliance with the insurgents paled into moral obligation, and was no longer implemented.

[66] Mulroy, *supra.*, p. 28.

[67] As but one instance: In 1812, in a "Seminole" raid and attack on the Kingsley plantation, approximately 40 Africans were liberated. Among these forty

John Horse, as he
appeared around 1840

Hon. Joshua R. Giddings
of Ohio

Major Gen. Jackson
circa 1820

with the inspiration of and assistance resulting from the successful Haitian revolution,[68] helps to explain how an insurrection plotted in Charleston, South Carolina in 1822 could have been deemed feasible by the plotters, and elicited the support of over 9,000 Africans in the area.

By 1822, almost all the captured Africans in the plantations surrounding Charleston had joined the revolt. Peter Poyas, among Vesey's lieutenants and said to be one of the great military and organizational geniuses of the early nineteenth century,[69] organized the revolt into separate cells under individual leaders.

That this revolt was not simply drawing on local forces in the Charleston area is indicated by the involvement of Gullah Jack, who was selected to lead the contingent from a coastal island near Charleston. Having been liberated during what is usually referred to as a "Seminole" raid and attack on Kingsley Plantation, and likely captured and re-enslaved at some point during the African War in Florida,[70]

Gullah Jack would have brought to the conspiracy an awareness of the African insurgency that had been taking place in Florida—and so would all other Africans who had been captured and re-enslaved. This connection would have tied the Vesey revolt into the fabric of the ongoing African insurrection.

Sketch of Indian & Negro towns on the Suwanee River

The date set for the uprising, July 24,1822, was advanced to June 16th when Vesey learned that one of the enslaved tied to the black church found out about the revolt and informed the authorities, who immediately increased patrols and began hauling in suspects for questioning. While he sent a messenger to inform the insurgents in St. John's Parish, a military patrol prevented him from leaving the city. Though there were

---

was Gullah Jack. Accounts of this man then appeared in Charleston, South Carolina in 1821, where he was purchased by Paul Pritchard. Gullah Jack was also a member of the African congregation along with Denmark Vesey. Just after Christmas of 1821, Vesey recruited Gullah Jack to be a lieutenant in the uprising that Vesey was planning for the city of Charleston and surrounding islands. Source: Marquetta L. Goodwine.

[68] See the Denmark Vesey section by Bernard Powers in ""De Ones Ya'll Kno' 'Bout" in Goodwine, *The Legacy of Ibo Landing, supra.*

[69] According to Richard Hooker, World Cultures Home Page, <http://www.wsu.edu:8000/-dee/ DIASPORA/ REBEL.htm>.

[70] Goodwine, *supra.*

an estimated 1,000 armed men prepared to strike on the appointed date, Denmark Vesey called off the attack, fearing an extensive defeat and reprisal.

The trials of the conspirators went on for 5 1/2 weeks. The defendants were divided into two groups: planners, those who had attended meetings, contributed money or showed no remorse after the initial hearing and a second group formed of all the rest. It was determined at the outset that the first group would be executed and the second deported—perhaps since little other alternative remained as to what to do with them. Jail for such numbers was impossible, as was mass execution. (An estimated 9,000 were involved in the conspiracy, only 67 were convicted of any offense. Denmark Vesey and 34 others were hanged.) The uprising itself may have confirmed that reintegrating recaptured Africans among the others was problematic.

THE SECOND PERIOD OF THE AFRICAN INSURGENCY

By 1834, some 10,000 men, a major part of the Regular Army of the United States, were concentrated in Florida.[71] What is traditionally called the Second Seminole War erupted again in 1835. It resulted from continuing U.S. efforts to force the Indians to abandon their alliance with the Africans, forcing them to leave lands in Florida committed to them by treaty in 1824, and to resettle amid their Creek enemies in Oklahoma. Typically, U.S. colonial expansion sought to expropriate the lands of the First Nations.

When Seminole Indian leaders were tricked into signing a treaty concerning their removal,[72] hostilities broke out.[73] It was a war which General Sidney Thomas Jesup, the commander of U.S. forces, viewed as "a negro and not an Indian war,"[74] although "the two races... are identified in interests and feelings."[75]

---

[71] Porter, *supra,* p. 82.

[72] Katz, *supra.,* p. 59.

[73] An additional cause of hostilities may have been the effort to humiliate Osceola in the eyes of the Gullah by the capture and re-enslavement of Morning Dew by slave-catchers while Osceola was having dinner with Thompson. Luring her captors into a compromising situation, Morning Dew killed them, then committed suicide. Osceola, overcome with grief and anger, had lain the blame at the feet of Thompson (described by Porter, p. 40, as "honest and conscientious") whom he felt not only had done nothing to save her, but might even have been complicit in her capture. *Thompson was shot and killed by Osceola's band after having been stalked for over a year in memory of his complicity in the plot to capture and re-enslave Osceola's wife.*

[74] Katz, *supra.,* p. 60.

[75] *ibid.,* p. 61.

The second period of the insurgency began with a series of African/First Nation victories (among them the victory over the Fort King Relief, termed the Dade Massacre)[76] in 1835, and over the U.S. army led by General Clinch at the Battle of the Withlacoochee.

The Victory over the Fort King Relief (The Dade Massacre) 1835

The relief forces of Major Francis L. Dade were en route to supplement forces at Fort King when the insurgents attacked them by surprise. According to Luis Pacheco, their African guide who escaped and later joined the allies, "There was a whole 'passel' of hound dogs in the troop"—possibly indicating that slave hunting was anticipated.[77] In the initial volley of shots, the officers were specifically targeted.[78] The U.S. forces responded with musket and cannon fire, until the cannon ammunition ran out. The final assault upon them was undertaken by "about fifty mounted black warriors."[79]

Customarily termed a 'massacre' rather than a battle by historians, this battle led to significant U.S. troop casualties: more than 100, compared with exile alliance losses of three.

The Battles of the Withlacoochee River, 1835

Porter provides a fascinating description of the Battles of Withlacoochee,[80] in which vastly outnumbered African and First Nations insurgents held the river against successive contingents of U.S. forces from December 1835, up to November 13th, 1836. This occurred when an overwhelming U.S. force led by General

---

[76] It should be remembered that by this time, the U.S. army had over 10,000 troops in Florida, in support of a U.S. policy determined to resettle the Indians and break the alliance between them and the Gullah. Dade's forces, albeit taken by surprise, had been at war with the exiles. This was not, however much the terminology might imply it, a "massacre of the innocents" but rather a military encounter in which one side made good use of the tactic of surprise.

[77] Porter, *supra,* p. 40. Italics added.

[78] Porter, *supra,* p. 42. The allied forces (though estimated by their opponents, of whom 3 survived, at some 800-1,000) were estimated by themselves at some 180 warriors. Porter describes 50 Africans who came forward to attack from behind the Seminole lines in such a way as to make them appear an encroaching contingent separate from those who had fought the U.S. forces until the U.S. guns were silenced. This neatly discredits Africans from victory, and ombfuscates the nature of the combatants.

[79] Porter, *supra,* p. 43.

[80] Porter, *supra,* pp. 44-62. Compare this to the differing account in Bland, 66 ff.

Seminole Battle Against Major Dade Forces in Florida
Original format: Engraving Creator: Blanchard, D.F.Creation date: 1836
Library of Congress, LC-USZ62-366

The 1836 wood engraving (left) was printed for D.F. Blanchard's narrative of the war, and is among the best-known representations of the conflict. The original caption offers the colonial perspective on the so-called "Dade Massacre" in Florida: "**Massacre of the Whites by the Indians and Blacks in Florida.** The above is intended to represent the horrid Massacre of the Whites in Florida, in December 1835, and January, February, March and April 1836, when near Four Hundred (including women and children) fell victim to the barbarity [strategic attack] of the Negroes and Indians."

While represented by modern scholarship as indicating "[Anglo-American] fears of African and Indian collusion", and as designed for the purpose of gaining early and strong support for the Anglo-American colonists' cause, the engraving actually attests to the extent of African leadership in the Seminole Wars, despite the fact that they were widely represented, then and now, as Indian wars.

Though the images portray African and Indian violence against the Anglo-American colonists, it is to be recalled that the Africans were fighting against their recapture, and against the institutions of enslavement, and the Indians were resisting the seizure of their lands, while the colonists were struggling to maintain slavery and to maintain and expand their occupation of the lands of American indigenous peoples. As expressed by J.B. Bird:

> Within hours, 105 U.S. soldiers lay dead. The Seminoles had lost only three warriors. For the first time in a genera-tion, they had dealt a deadly blow to the army of Andrew Jackson—the army that massacred 300 blacks and Indians at the Negro Fort (1816), that burned and pillaged Seminole towns in the First Seminole War (1817-18), and that brought American statehood and slavery to the once-free wilderness of Florida (1821).*

*Bird, J.B. "The largest slave rebellion in U.S. history." Rebellion: John Horse and the Black Seminoles, First Black Rebels to Beat American Slavery, 2005 (accessed March 16, 2006). <http://www.johnhorse.com>.

Massacre of Major Dade and his Command

Battle of Lake Okeechobee

"Burning of the town Pilak-li-ka-ha by Gen. Eustis." "Pilak-li-ka-ha was also known as "Abraham's town," having served as his home and headquarters since the 1820s.

"Attack of the Seminoles on the block house."

Call and augmented by Creeks whom the U.S. had promised the booty of any blacks they might capture.

In the first battle on December 31st, 1835, the exile forces were not only able to prevent six companies of the U.S. Fourth Infantry and a regiment of Louisiana volunteers from crossing the Withlacoochee River, but nearly succeeded (but for a change in the wind direction) in overcoming their erected defenses on the other side of the river. Had it not been for the arrival of reinforcements under General Cinch, the demoralized and famished U.S. army contingent would surely have succumbed—

Arrival of the So. Ca. Dragoons at the Withlacoochee

either to the superior and innovative military tactics of the insurgents, or to starvation.

As it was, having gained vital time for the evacuation of their communities, the insurgents withdrew further south. In this battle, the exile forces lost three men, with five wounded, while Gaines' losses were five dead and forty-six wounded.[81]

After a period of recuperation for his troops at Camp Izard, "General Gaines soon left Florida, issuing a statement that the enemy had been 'met, beaten, and forced to sue for peace.' His men had not crossed the Withlacoochee River, and the allied tribespeople and blacks still held the region."[82]

These U.S. troops did not succeed in crossing the Withlacoochee until nearly a full year thereafter. The vastly outnumbered insurgents had taken the only recourse that common sense demanded: they had melted away to the south. While the U.S. forces could be said to have eventually succeeded in crossing the river, they cannot be said to have won these battles. The encounter at Wahoo Swamp which followed thereafter, though it occasioned heavy losses among the allied insurgents (some 620 men of which 200 were African, still fought the contending forces on opposite sides of the Withlacoochee.) This battle was officially proclaimed by the U.S. side as "a brilliant day..."[83]

---

[81] Extensive sources are cited by Porter, *supra,* p. 52.
[82] Porter, *supra.,*p. 52.
[83] Porter, *supra.,* p. 64.

The U.S. General Jesup, commander of the Florida Territory, endeavored to break the African/ Indian alliance by eliminating independent black communities in Florida and promoting black slaveholding among the Indians. When this in turn proved largely unsuccessful, the next option was removal. The Jackson administration sought an immediate removal treaty with the Seminoles.[84] This period of the conflict was ultimately terminated by a treaty which sought to remove these warrior communities to parts of the West [85]

The dilemma which the U.S. faced was this: how to rid Florida of the free African communities. Given the legacy of the Denmark Vessey Revolt, General Jesup could not propose to allow the dissemination of these free Africans (trained in the use of firearms and accustomed to freedom) to be returned to or placed on southern enslavement plantations. Surely they would take the lead in future revolts of the captive Africans.[86] On the other hand, it was clearly exceedingly costly and difficult to bring the insurgents to their knees, or to sufficiently decimate their numbers militarily. Somewhere along the line, acquiescence to removal had to be the best of the scanty options. Accordingly, Jesup commenced a series of negotiations. On March 6, 1837, a treaty was made with "the Seminole nation of Indians and their *allies,*" undoubtedly referring to the Africans. Article 5 stated that:

General Jessup

> Major General Jesup, in behalf of the United States, agreed that the Seminole and *their allies,* who come in and emigrate west, shall be secure in their lives and property; that *their negroes,* their bona fide property, shall also accompany them West.[87]

The wording, a master stroke in diplomacy, sought to satisfy Africans demands for emancipation, while at the same time, by calling

[84] Mulroy, *supra.*, p. 27.
[85] Seminole agent Thompson believed that a major cause of Seminole hostility to removal was "the influence which it is said the negroes, [said by Thompson to be] the very slaves in the nation, have over the Indians." Mulroy, *supra,* p. 28.
[86] Mulroy, *supra.*, p. 31.
[87] Porter, *supra.*, p. 77.

them slaves of Seminoles, catering to the Florida settlers' concerns that the Africans should not be emancipated, negotiated with, or spoken of in any way other than as somebody's property.

But even African removal—if it occurred in association with any hint of emancipation—did not remove the potential threat of Africans in freedom on the same continent in those areas where Africans were still captured and enslaved.

The Florida settlers forced Jesup to return to hammering the Indian contingent for the surrender of the Africans, something of course Jesup knew they did not have the power to do even if they were willing. Jesup returned to his efforts to break the alliance, and to turn the allies against each other.

In the face of ongoing resistance, in February 1838, through the use of African emissaries to the leader (John Hors) of the major African communities, Jesup ultimately promised "freedom and protection" if they would separate from the Indians and surrender, accepting to be sent to the west. As Mulroy noted: "*Black emancipation and removal suddenly had become the policy of the United States army.*" But to disguise this, it had been necessary to view all African insurgents (perhaps four-fifths of whom were runaways or their descendants), as property of the Seminole Indians. Whether this was true (in any manner in the present or past) was immaterial to the politico-legal necessity to assert that this indeed was the situation, and thereby camouflage the noxious notion of African freedom.

The Battle of Lake Okeechobee

What General Jesup couldn't accomplish in battle, he accomplished by trickery and deceit. When the Seminole Indian Chief, Osceola, had approached him with a contingent of some seventy hostages, to further negotiate the terms of peace, rather than negotiate, Jesup captured him.

While Osceola languished in prison at Fort Moultrie, his life slipping away due to illness at the age of 34, some twenty or so of those captured with him escaped to freedom, led by John Horse and Wild Cat. They were pursued by Colonel Zachary Taylor with a force of 70 Delaware Indians, 180 Tennessee volunteer sharpshooters and 800 U.S. soldiers. According to William Loren Katz:

> The first shot had hardly been fired when the Delawares deserted. Tennessee riflemen plunged ahead intending to wipe out the Seminoles and a

withering fire brought down their commissioned officers and then their noncomissioned officers. The Tennesseans fled.

When the U.S. regulars were ordered forward, pinpoint accurate fire brought down, according to Colonel Taylor, 'every officer, with one exception, as well as most of the noncommissioned officers' and left 'but four... untouched...' The battle of Lake Okeechobee became the most decisive upset:

> the U.S. suffered in more than four decades of warfare in Florida. But since the Seminoles had finally abandoned the battle scene [knowing they were no match for hundreds of soldiers], Colonel Taylor claimed a victory.[88]

Typical of the victories of U.S. forces against the African/Indian alliance, the commander on the U.S. side declared victory as his enemy melted into the bush.

Eventually, without sources from whom to secure arms and ammunition or the protection of political borders, the exile alliance forces would be outgunned by the superior arms, logistics, and demographic and political situation of the U.S. army. Nonetheless, during this stage of the African War, which was essentially a defensive action, there emerged many outstanding leaders among the insurgents, whose names might well join the historical roster of those who resisted the oppression of African Americans and Indians over the centuries.

These names appeared again and again in official dispatches over time, yet largely remain unknown to the peoples who might most wish to recall them. The names of the African Americans such as Abraham [Ibrahim], John Horse [Juan Cavallo], Francisco Menéndez and Garçon (commanders of Fort Mose/Prospect Bluff), Luis Pacheco, and of First Nations Chiefs, such as Osceola, Alligator, Wild Cat, Talmieco-Hadjo, Arpeika, TigerTail, and many others will one day find their place in history alongside other great freedom fighters.

These were among the leaders who formed an alliance of resistance between African American and American indigenous peoples, which was renewed again and again for over a century, despite the onslaught of U.S. troops in the field, and a barrage of ploys put forward by governments, military officers and U.S. Indian agents and allies. These were the leaders who formed the soil which nourished

---

[88] *ibid.*, p. 67.

later leaders—Marcus Garvey, Elijah Muhammad, W.E.B. DuBois, etc. —who in turn provided the soil for the contemporary martyred leaders of our day: Martin Luther King and Malcolm X. These were the forefathers of African American resistance to captivity with the intent to enslave.

Seeing only defeat in remaining in Florida, elements of the African/ Indian alliance regrouped first in Oklahoma with the most steadfast of their fighters, then went on to Coahuila, Mexico, where they once again benefited from the protection of a political boundary and a well-wishing state.[93] The exiles established themselves close to the small town of Santa Rosa. Unable to rid themselves of their predilection for oppression and the enslaviement of others, U.S. settlers from Texas organized two expeditions against them for the purpose of seizing and enslaving them. These efforts met with armed resistance. The settlers were reported by Texas newspapers to have returned without "accomplishing the objective intended and... with their own numbers diminished in conflict" against the African exiles.

Even at this point, the African insurgency had not collapsed to the point of mere self-defense. The Texas press reported some six months later that "Indians" (the disguise for African American and Indian insurgency) had crossed the frontier, and destroyed plantations, burned buildings, and set enslaved African Americans free. As Giddings noted, African American and Indian guerrillas appeared ready, even at what might have appeared the culmination of their epic efforts, to make war on all who fought for slavery.[94] The descendants of the African exiles never signed or voluntarily surrendered to the U.S. government.[95]

CONCLUSION

To regard these wars as simply regional struggles is to vastly understate their impact. This insurgency challenged the very existence of the institutions of colonization and enslavement. It remained a constant negation of the notion propagated by plantation owners: that the captured and enslaved Africans acquiesced to and were benefiting from what was called the civilizing and Christianizing influence of their captors. Within the span of two short decades, with the passage of the Emancipation Proclamation after a civil war in which African Americans once again arose en masse to fight for their freedom, the entire enslavement system crumbled.

These African ancestors left Afro-Carolinians and all African Americans with a history of which they can be rightfully proud. In no prior historical instance—whether in ancient Egypt, in Africa under Sundiata Kiata, or that faced by the ancient Jews of Masada, or the

"BILLY BOWLEGS" AND HIS RETINUE.

Abraham (center, standing) pictured with the Billy Bowlegs delegation to Washington in 1853, as published in *The Illustrated London News*, May 23, 1853. (This engraving is sometimes identified as a depiction of the delegation that travelled to Washington in 1826.) *Florida Photographic Collection*. http://www.johnhorse.com/trail/01/c/11zz.htm. NOTE: The reason why most of the leaders in this image are Indians is that the US government refused to meet with the African leadership, as such. Although one of the most important among the leadership, Abraham was forced to attend the meeting in guise of a translator.

contemporary Palestinians—had any people fought more gallantly for freedom and self-determination under more difficult circumstances.

Thousands of miles from Africa at a historical period when communication with their homeland was absolutely impossible, forcibly relocated to a continent where they were strangers and without historical allies, but allying with unknown nations whose languages and customs were alien to theirs just as their own individual African languages and customs were alien to each other. They were designated as slaves by a technologically powerful nation of people heretofore unknown to them, who refused to speak to them, write about them or deal with them in any other capacity than as someone's slave. Nonetheless, individuals from these different African tribes mounted a resistance so fierce that they were able to forestall the will of a vastly superior power for over a century, and instill in the minds of the most stout of the racist U.S. colonists the fear or realization that the captured Africans could not be held indefinitely. Assuredly, if one were to ask where the true American revolution for freedom and self-determination took place, the answer would have to include the African/ First Nations insurgency

When we contrast the collective efforts of the African Americans with that of the collective U.S. colonist efforts of the time, we cannot help but ask which stood most in line with the spirit of the celebrated U.S. Declaration of Independence: "We take these truths to be self-evident: that all men are created equal..."

The historians tell us: from 1739 onwards through the African-First Nations Alliance, the U.S. Government sought to enter the Africans in the enslavement process. After the American Revolution of 1776, the U.S. government abandoned its promises to the African American by accepting the dismantlement of Reconstruction and the racist premises of segregation. It acquiesced to the institutionalization of gross domination and oppression.

Whatever the future may hold, this much, surely, should be reclaimed and recognized as a key axiom of African American history: that the African and Indian War played a major role in convincing the U.S. colonial power structure that the institution of enslavement and colonialism has no future; that those it captured could be counted on to mount unending resistance. Indeed, it might be said that it was here in America, during the Gullah War, that the globalized institution of enslavement as a system facilitating capitalist development was halted—not due to the "inutility of slave labor," but because those who were enslaved made it dear that the enslaved did not accept their captivity, and that in all the ways that were possible, they would rebel.

CHAPTER THREE

"'TWAS A NEGRO WHO TAUGHT THEM"

A NEW LOOK AT AFRICAN LABOR IN EARLY SOUTH CAROLINA*

[demonstrating the captive African population's logistic capacity
to mount a successful anti-enslavement resistance]

PETER H. WOOD

When Col. John Barnwell of South Carolina laid siege to the
stronghold of the Tuscarora Indians in the spring of 1712, he noticed
a special ingenuity in the fortification. "I immediately viewed the Fort
with a prospective glass and found it strong", the commander wrote.
Not only were there impressive trenches, bastions, and earthworks
to ward off attack, but heavy tree limbs had been placed around the
fort making any approach difficult and hiding innumerable "large reeds
& canes to run into peoples's legs." What struck Barnwell particularly
was the fact that, according to the fort's occupants, "it was a runaway
[African-American, so-called Seminole] taught them to fortify thus."
At that early date, the Africans and English had lived in the region for
scarcely a generation, and it is not likely that this enslaved African,
identified only as "Harry," had been born in Carolina. Instead it seems
probable that he had grown up in Africa and had lived in South Carolina
before he was "[transported] into Virginia for roguery &... fled to the
Tuscaruros" (*Virginia Magazine*, July 1898, 44-45). If Harry's African
know-how caught the South Carolina commander off guard, it may
also startle modern historians, for this obscure incident exemplifies

---

* This work was originally published in the *Journal of Asian and African Studies*,
IX, 3-4 July and October 1974. An earlier version of this paper was read to the
Organization of American Historians in 1972. Material appearing here is presented
in a fuller context in Peter H. Wood, *Black Majority: Negroes in Colonial South
Carolina from 1670 through the Stono Rebellion*. (New York 1974). An abridged
version is included here as an indication of the forced African immigrant
population's logistical potential to mount a successful anti-colonial resistance.
The text has been terminologically updated to conform to guidelines and usage
agreed upon by the UN Committee on the Elimination of Racial Discrimination, following
the World Conference on Racism. [*Editor*]

an intriguing aspect of Afro American history which has not yet been adequately explored.

Colonial South Carolina is an excellent place to begin searching the cultural baggage of early forced immigrants for what anthropologists have termed "carryovers". More captured Africans entered North America through Charleston (called Charlestown until 1783) than through any other single port, and no other mainland region had so high a ratio of Africans to Europeans throughout the eighteenth century as did South Carolina. Early migrants from Barbados and other places where enslavement was well-established brought captured African workers with them when they could afford it. In the initial years after 1670, however, most English settlers hoped to meet the colony's intensive labor needs in other ways. Attempts were made to procure a steady supply of European workers and to employ neighboring Indians on a regular basis, but neither of these sources could meet the demand. Within half a century Africans constituted a majority of the settlement's population, and additional forced immigrants were being imported regularly from Africa.

That such a large percentage of early South Carolinians were African-Americans has never been thoroughly explained, though basic contributing factors have long been recognized: European racism, colonial precedent, and the proximity of the African trading routes. No other workers were available for such extended terms, in such large numbers, at so low a rate. Indeed, such labor was, so it has always seemed, almost inevitable. And perhaps for this very reason, the question of whether Africans brought with them any inherited knowledge and practical skills from the African continent has seemed irrelevant to Anglo-American historians. Though the anthropologist Melville Herskovits challenged "The Myth of the Negro Past" more than thirty years ago, the American historian has tended to uphold the legend that blacks had no prior cultures of any consequence, or that if they did, little could have survived the traumatic Middle Passage (Herskovits 1941). (McPherson (1971 :32-39) indicates that a few Anglo-American historians have considered some carryovers, but little attention has been given to the importation of any practical kinds of cultural information.) Africans, according to this approach, were forced to immigrate in spite of being thoroughly unskilled (or perhaps in part *because* of it). And it followed from this that the central chore which faced those Europeans who saw themselves as masters was one of patient and one-sided education, so that "ignorant" Africans could be taught to manage simple tasks.

Yet in actuality something very different took place. In the earliest years of colonization, Africans demonstrated skills and talents that the Anglo-Americans were unwilling to admit. Within several decades the necessity for labor of any sort led to an increase in the size and diversity of the African population, and a further variety of African skills emerged which were strikingly appropriate to the lowland frontier. Africans, therefore, were far from being the passive objects of Anglo-Carolinian instruction. Indeed, a process of mutual education took place among the Africans themselves, despite initial language problems. And many of these workers, regardless of their legal status, occasionally ended up teaching those who saw themselves as their superiors. Africans, as will be made clear, often proved knowledgeable and competent in areas where Europeans remained disdainful or ignorant. Hence the problem faced by Anglo-Carolinians during the first and second generation of settlement was less one of imparting knowledge to unskilled workers than of controlling for their own ends African expertise which could be and was, as in Harry's case, readily turned against them.

Though hitherto unacknowledged, the comparative advantages which Africans possessed over Europeans in this New World setting can be seen in a variety of different ways. South Carolina, first of all, was in a different geographic zone from England and from all the earlier English colonies in mainland North America. This fact was pleasing to Anglo-Carolinian settlers on one level, but disconcerting on another, and they were slow to make the adjustments necessary for life in a somewhat alien semi-tropical region. John Lawson, an amateur naturalist who explored the Carolinas at the start of the eighteenth century, commented that if English colonists "would be so curious as to make nice Observations of the Soil, and other remarkable Accidents, they would soon be acquainted with the Nature of the Earth and Climate, and be better qualified to manage their Agriculture to more Certainty." But he went on to admit, as would Jefferson and others after him, that Europeans seemed to become less careful and observant rather than more so in the unfamiliar environment of the American South (Lawson 1967 (1709) : 80,81).

West Africans, on the other hand, were not only more accustomed to the flora and fauna of a subtropical climate generally, but they possessed an orientation toward what Levi-Strauss has called "extreme familiarity with their biological environment,... passionate attention ... to it and ... precise knowledge of it" (Levi-Strauss 1966: 5). Even prior to the 1600's Africans had established a reputation for being able to subsist off the land more readily than

Europeans in the Southeast. A century before the founding of Carolina, when Africans were sent to work on the fortifications at St. Augustine, a Spanish official had written approvingly, "With regard to their food, they will display diligence as they seek it in the country, without any cost to the royal treasure" (*Colonial Records of Spanish Florida*, 1930:315). Instances of black self-sufficiency* (like instances of Indian assistance) made a lasting impression upon less well acclimated Anglo-Carolinians, and as late as 1775 we find an influential English text repeating the doctrine that in Carolina, "The common idea ... is, that one Indian, or dextrous [African], will, with his gun and netts, get as much game and fish as five families can eat; and the [Africans] support themselves in provisions, besides raising ... staples" (Land 1969:67).

By far the largest number of people entering South Carolina during the colonial period came from West Africa, and, in the course of a century of immigration, items indigenous to parts of that vast region were transported with them. For example, though white colonists would debate at length which European should receive credit for introducing the first bag of rice seed,[1] it is possible that successful rice cultivation followed the arrival of seeds aboard a ship from Africa.[2] Often the botanical imprecision of contemporary Englishmen makes it hard to say exactly which plants were introduced and when. Semantic confusion about Guinea corn and Indian corn provides a case in point. Maurice Mathews reported during the initial summer of settlement that along with Indian corn, "Guiney Corne growes very well here, but this being ye first I euer planted ye perfection I will not Aver till ye Winter doth come in" (South Carolina Historical Society, Collections, V, 333). This grain or some subsequent variety clearly took hold, for in the next generation Lawson reported Guinea corn to be thriving; he noted it was used mostly for hogs and poultry, while adding that many Africans ate "nothing but" Indian corn (with salt) (Lawson 1967 (1709) : 81). A definition offered by Mark Catesby in 1743 reveals that Indian and Guiney corn had become interchangeable in English texts, if not in actual fact:

> Milium Indicum. Bunched Guinea Corn. But little
> of this grain is propagated, and that chiefly by

---

* It was this attention and knowledge of that environment which permitted them and their Indian allies to successfully escape to freedom, survive off the land, and successfully deflect the U.S. army's efforts to re-capture them.

Africans, who make bread of it, and boil it in like
manner of firmety. Its chief use is for feeding fowls...
It was at first introduced from Africa by the Africans
(Catesby 1743, appendix, xviii).

Catesby also recorded "The Leg-worm, or Guinea-worm"
among the "insects" he found in Carolina, and Lawson listed among
varieties of musk-melon a "guinea melon" which may have come
from Africa. Others mentioned the "guinea fowl" or "guinea hen," a
domesticated West African bird which was introduced into North
America during the eighteenth century. Henry Laurens of Charleston
(like George Washington of Mount Vernon) acquired seed for "guinea
grass," a tall African grass used for fodder (Lawson 1967 (1709) :
81-83; Mathews, II, 1193).

The West African and Carolinian climates were similar
enough so that even where flora and fauna were not literally
transplanted, a great deal of knowledge proved transferable. African
cultures placed a high priority on their extensive pharmacopoeia,
and details known through oral tradition were readily transported to
the New World. For example, expertise included familiarity with a
variety of herbal antidotes and abortives (Vansina 1971: 443; Curtin
1968 : 215). A South Carolina African was freed from captivity and
awarded one hundred pounds per year for life from the Assembly for
revealing his antidote to certain poisons; "Cesar's Cure" was printed
in the *South Carolina Gazette* and appeared occasionally in local
almanacs for more than thirty years (*S.C. Gazette*, May 9, 1750;
Webber 1914: 78; On Caesar, cf. Duncan 1972: 64-66).

Although certain medicinal knowledge was confined to
specially experienced Africans(some of whom were known openly
as "doctors"), almost all Africans showed a general familiarity with
lowland plants. Africans regularly gathered berries and wild herbs for
their own use and for sale. John Brickell noted of Africans in Carolina,
for example, that "on Sundays, they gather Snake-Root, otherwise it
would be excessive dear if the Christians were to gather it" (Brickell
1911 (1737): 275). The economic benefits to be derived from workers
with such horticultural skills were not lost upon speculative Europeans.
In 1726 Richard Ludlam urged the collection and cultivation of special
plants upon which the cochineal beetle (an insect used to produce
red dye) might feed and grow. According to Ludlam:

Two or Three [Africans] will gather as many
Spontaneous Plants in one day, as will in another
Day regularly Plant Ten Acres, by the Same hands

and for the Quantity of Plants Growing here on the
Banks of River & in the multitudes of Islands on the
Sea Coasts, I can Safely Assure you... Thousands
of Acres might, at a Little Charge, be Stock with
them.[3]

   Bringing a greater awareness of the environment with them,
forced African immigrants were better able to profit from contact with
native Indians than were the equally foreign Anglo-Carolinian colonists.
A variety of plants and processes were known to both West African
and southeastern American cultures, and such knowledge must have
been shared and reinforced upon contact. Gourds, for example served
as milk pails along the Gambia River in much the same way
calabashes had long provided water buckets beside the Ashley[4] (Grant
1968: 24; Lawson 1967 (1709): 149). The creation of elaborate
baskets, boxes, and mats from various reeds and grasses was familiar
to both black and red (Lawson 1967 (1709) : 195-196), and South
Carolina's strong basket-weaving tradition, still plainly visible on the
roadsides north of Charleston, undoubtedly represents an early fusion
of African and Indian skills (Smith 1936: 71).
   The palmetto, symbol of the novel landscape for arriving
Europeans, was well known to Africans and Indians for its useful
leaf. They made fans and brooms from these leaves and may well
have entered into competition with Bermudians who were already
exporting baskets and boxes made of woven palmetto (Lawson 1967
(1709): 14; Corry 1968 (1807): 66). An authority on Carolina furniture
writes that "The very early inventories frequently mention Palmetto
chairs or Palmetto-bottom chairs" (Burton 1955: 36-37). The skill
and labor behind these traditional items may well have been primarily
African, as suggested by one surviving mortgage. In 1729 Thomas
Holton, a producer of chairs and couches, listed as collateral three
captured Africans, by trade Chairmakers (Wills, Inventories, and
Miscellaneous Records, 1729-1731: 27).
   Through the first two generations of settlement Indians were
common among the Africans in lowland Carolina, both as enslaved
and as free neighbors (Cf. Dundes 1965: 207-219; Hudson 1971).
But the number of Indians steadily declined, and as their once-
formidable know-how dissipated it was the Africans who assimilated
the largest share of their lore and who increasingly took over their
responsibilities as "pathfinders" in the Southern wilderness. Blacks
became responsible for transporting goods to market by land and
water and for ferrying passengers and livestock. From the first years
of settlement the primary means of direct communication between

colonists holding captured Africans was through letters carried by these very Africans. Charleston set up a local post office at the beginning of the eighteenth century, and by 1740 there was a weekly mail going south toward the new colony of Georgia and a monthly post overland to the north via Georgetown and Cape Fear, but with the exception of these minimal services the responsibility for delivering letters in the region fell entirely to African boatmen and runners throughout the colonial period (Cooper and McCord, II, 188-189; *S.C. Gazette*, September 17, 1737; May 3, 1739; November 20, 1740).

There is no better illustration of Anglo-Carolinian reliance upon African knowledge of the environment than the fact that captured Africans became quite literally the guides of Anglo-Carolinians. Contemporary records give adequate testimony. John Lawson, travelling from the Ashley to the Santee by canoe at the start of the eighteenth century, relates that at one point a local doctor "sent [an African] to guide us over the Head of the Swamp" (Lawson 1967 (1709): 20-21). A public official such as the Provost Marshal would sometimes be provided with an African boy "to Show him the way" between plantations (*Journal of the Commons House of Assembly, 1726-1727*, 119). In October 1745 an Anglo-Carolinian traveller coming from Philadelphia recorded in his Journal: "had [an African] to guide us the Road being Intricate" (Pemberton *Diary*, 1745), and in the same month a minister of the Society for the Propagation of the Gospel wrote that his parishioners had urged him to secure the family of three Africans.

> I consented [he wrote] not knowing full well the ways and management of country affair[s] .., and was obliged also by extream necessity to buy 3 horses with bridles and saddles, one for me, another for my wife, and the other for [an African] servant, for it would be impossible for me to go through the Parish between the woods without a Guide (Boschi 1949 (1745) 185).

In 1770 William De Brahm would observe that Africans, besides being stationed at the plantation gates to offer hospitality to travellers, were often sent with departing guests "to cut down small trees in the way of carriages, to forward and guide through unfrequented forests, ... (and) to set them over streams, rivers and creeks" (Weston 1856: 179). It is not an unrelated fact that ever since colonial times Africans have commonly served as guides to

Anglo-Carolinian and other sportsmen in the Sea Islands and throughout the coastal South (Cf. Crum, Chapter IV).

It is striking to find African familiarity with the land more than matched by familiarity with the coastal sea. Although Europeans were unrivalled as the builders and navigators of oceangoing ships, there was little in the background of most Anglo immigrants to prepare them for negotiating the labyrinth of unchanneled swamps and tidal marshes which interlaced the lowland settlement. Afro-Americans drew on a different heritage. Some Africans had scarcely seen deep water before their forced passage to America, and none had sailed in ocean vessels; yet many had grown up along rivers or beside the ocean and were far more at home in this element than most Europeans, for whom a simple bath was still exceptional (Cf. Turberville 1929: 126, for history of English bathing). Lawson, describing the awesome shark, related "how Some Negro's and others, that can swim and drive well, go naked into the Water, with a Knife in their Hand, and fight the Shark, and very commonly kill him" (Lawson 1967 (1709): 158). Similarly the alligator, a fresh-water reptile which horrified Europeans (since it was unfamiliar and could not be killed with a gun), was readily handled by Africans used to protecting their stock from African crocodiles (Grant 1968: 13, 23; see also Schaw 1922: 149-151).

Most importantly, a large number of Africans were more at home than Anglo-Carolinians in dugout canoes, and these slender boats were the central means of transportation in South Carolina for several generations while roads and bridges were still too poor and infrequent for easy land travel.[5] Small canoes were hollowed from single cypress logs by Africans or Indians, or by whites whom they instructed in the craft.[6] To make the larger canoe known as a pettiauger two or three trees were used, giving the boat additional beam for cargo without significantly increasing its draft; fifty to one hundred barrels of tar or rice [and eventually, war supplies] could be ferried along shallow creeks and across tidal shoals in such vessels.

These boats were frequently equipped with one or even two portable masts for sailing and often ventured onto the open ocean (Lawson 1967 (1709), 103, 104, 107; Clontes 1926: 16-35; Cf. Mc.Kusick 1960). Their design may have represented a syncretic blend between European, Caribbean, and Indian styles on the one hand, and on the other hand diverse coastal traditions from West Africa, where cypress wood was used to fashion both round and flat bottomed craft (Batutah 1929 [1325-1354]: 333; Hakluyt 1904: 18; see also Wax 1968: 474, 478). African crews, directed by an African "patron", managed these boats, and many of their earliest rowing songs were apparently remnants recalled from Africa (McCrady 1899: 516; Fisher 1953: 8).

The fact that dexterity in handling cypress canoes was an art brought from Africa is underscored by an advertisement for a runaway in the Virginia colony. The notice concerned "a new [African] Fellow of small Stature" from Bonny on the coast of Nigeria; it stated that "he calls himself Bonna, and says he came from a Place of that name in the Ibo Country, in Africa, where he served in the Capacity of a Canoe Man" (*Virginia Gazette*, December 24, 1772). In South Carolina Africans were often advertised in terms of their abilities on the water: "a very good Sailor, and used for 5 years to row in boats, ... a Lad chiefly used to row in boats," "a fine strong [African] Man, that has been used to the Sea, which he is very fit for, or to go in a Pettiaugua," "all fine Fellows in boats or Pettiau's". So many Africans brought these skills with them, or learned their seamanship in the colony from other Africans, that African familiarity with boating was accepted as axiomatic among Anglo-Carolinians. In 1741, when Henry Bedon advertised two African men "capable to go in a Pettiauger" who had been "going by the Water above 10 Years," he added that the pair "understands their Business" (*S.C. Gazette*, April 6, 1734; April 11, 1739; January 31, 1743; February 18, 1741).

"Their business" often included fishing, and it is not surprising that in the West Indian and southern colonies Africans quickly proved able to supply both themselves and European colonists with fish (Wax 1968: 475-476). In Charleston, an entire class of African "Fishing [men]" had emerged early in the eighteenth century, replacing local Indians as masters of the plentiful waters (*S.C. Gazette*, November 5, 1737). (For an excellent discussion of fishing slaves as a privileged subgroup, see Price 1968.) "There is .... Good fishing all along this Coast, especially from October till Christmas," wrote James Sutherland who commanded Johnson's Fort overlooking Charleston harbor during the 1730's, adding (perhaps with fisherman's license), "I've known two [Africans] take between 14 & 1500 Trouts above 3 feet long, wch make an excellent dry fish" (Coe Papers, undated). A French visitor whose ship anchored not far from Johnson's Fort early in the next century found himself "in the midst of twenty-five dugouts,"

> each containing four [Africans] who were having excellent fishing, such as one might well desire on the eve of Good Friday. Ten minutes doesn't go by without there being hauled into the dugout fish weighing from twelve to fifteen pounds. After they

are taken on the line, they are pulled up to the level
of the sea where one of the black fishermen sticks
them with a harpoon (Montlzun 1948: 136; see also
Price 1968: 1372).

Skill with hooks and harpoons was complemented by other
techniques more common in Africa and the Caribbean than in Europe.
The poisoning of streams to catch fish was known in West Africa
(Fyfe 1964 : 96), and fish drugging was also practised in the West
Indies, first by Island Caribs and later by enslaved Africans. They
dammed up a stream or inlet and added an intoxicating mixture of
quicklime and plant juices to the water. They could then gather
inebriated but edible fish from the pool almost at will (Price 1968:
1366, 1372; Quigley 1956: 508-525). Inhabitants of South Carolina
in the early eighteenth century exploited a similar tactic, for in 1726
the Assembly charged that "many persons in this Province do often
use the pernicious practice of poisoning the creeks in order to catch
great quantity of fish," *(Statutes*, III, 270; the misdemeanor seems
to have continued; cf. *S.C. Gazette*, April 6, 1734).

West Africans may also have imported the art of net casting,
which became an established tradition in the tidal shallows of Carolina.
The doctor aboard an American vessel carrying captured Africans off
the Gold Coast in the mid-eighteenth century recorded in his journal:
"It is impossible to imagine how very dextrous the [Africans] are in
catching fish with a net, this morning I watch'd one man throw one of
3 yards deep, and hale it in himself with innumerable fish" (Wax 1968:
474; see also Whitten and Szwed, pictorials, 11th p.). Weighted
drawstring nets, like the dugout canoes from which they were cast,
may have represented the syncretic blend of several ancient Atlantic
fishing traditions (Price 1968: 1374). The men who could handle nets
could also mend them; in 1737 a runaway (Seminole?) named Moses
was reported to be "well known in Charlestown, having been a Fisherman
there for some time, & hath been often employed in knitting of Nets"
(*S.C. Gazette*, November 5, 1737). The prevalence of African
commercial fishermen in the Southeast, as in the Caribbean, continued
long after the end of the enslavement system, and Africans who man
shrimpboats in present-day Carolina earn their living at a calling familiar
to many of their West African forebears.[7]

No single industry was more important to the early
settlement in South Carolina than the raising of livestock. While
the first generation of Englishmen experimented unsuccessfully with
such strange crops as grapes, olives, cotton, rice, indigo, and ginger
in the hopes of finding an appropriate staple, their livelihood depended

in large measure upon the cattle and hogs that could be raised with a minimum of labor. Beef and pork were in great demand in the West Indies, and these at least were items which the English had long produced. But even here there was an unfamiliar element. According to traditional European patterns of animal husbandry, farmers confined their cows in pastures, milked them regularly, and slaughtered them annually. Since winter fodder was limited, Europeans maintained only enough stock through the cold months to replenish their herds in the following spring. This practice made little sense in a region where cattle could "feed themselves perfectly well at no cost whatever" (Thibou 1683) throughout the year. Stock grew lean, but rarely starved in South Carolina's mild winters. Colonists therefore might build up large herds with little effort, a fact which could benefit the settlement but which dismayed the Proprietors in London. It has been "our designe", they stated indignantly, "to have Planters there and not graziers" (South Carolina Historical Society *Collections*, V, 437-438).

Africans, however, had no such disdain for open grazing, and many of the captured Africans entering South Carolina after 1670 may have had experience in tending large herds. Melville Herskovits, along with others, has pointed out that although domesticated cattle were absent from the Congo region due to the presence of the tse-tse fly, such animals were common along much of the African coast to the north and west. Stock was even traded for export on occasion. In 1651, for example, the English Guinea Company, precursor of the Royal African Company, instructed a captain to barter liquor at the Gambia River for a "Cargo of [Africans] or Cattel" to be carried to Barbados. People of the Gambia region, the area for which South Carolina slave dealers expressed a steady preference, were expert horsemen and herders. English visitors expressed high admiration for their standards of cleanliness with respect to dairy products, and contemporary descriptions of local animal husbandry bear a striking resemblance to what would later appear in Carolina. Herds grazed on the savannahs bordering the river and in the low-lying paddy fields when the rice crop was off; at night stock was tethered within a cattlefold and guarded by several armed men (Herskovits 1930: 67, 72, 73; Donnan 1930-1935, I, 129; Grant 1968: 24-25).

As early as the 1670's there is evidence of absentee investors relying upon Africans to develop herds of cattle in Carolina.[8] Even when the Anglo-Carolinian owner lived within the province, the care of his livestock often fell to an African. The African would build a small "cowpen" in some remote region, attend the calves and guard the grazing stock at night. When Denys Omahone sold a fifty-acre tract to a new colonist arrival in the 1680's the property contained, besides the Indians who still inhabited it, four calves, three steers, five sows, one boar and an African who took care of these animals, to whom he referred by the name of "Cato" (South Carolina Archives, Miscellaneous Records A, 1682-1690; 318-319)...

At first the Carolina settlement occupied a doubly colonial status, struggling to supply provisions to other English colonies.[9] The development of a trade in naval stores soon enabled the settlement to become a staple producer in its own right, but it was the cultivation of rice as an export commodity which came to dominate Carolina life in the course of the eighteenth century. Despite its eventual prominence, the mastery of this grain took more than a generation, for rice was a crop about which Englishmen, even those who had lived in the Caribbean, knew nothing at all. Immigrants from elsewhere in northern Europe were equally ignorant, and local Indians who gathered small quantities of wild rice had little to teach them.

In contrast to Europeans, Africans from the West Coast of Africa were widely familiar with rice planting. Ancient speakers of a Proto-Bantu language in the sub-Sahara region are known to have cultivated the crop (McCall 1964: 69). An indigenous variety (*Oryza glaberrima*) was a staple in the western rain-forest regions long before Portuguese and French navigators introduced Asian and American varieties of *O. sativa* in the 1500's. The northernmost English factory on the coast, James Fort in the Gambia River, was in a region where rice was grown in paddies along the riverbanks (Herskovits 1930; Donnan 1930-1935 : I; Grant 1968 : 24-25). In the Congo-Angola region, which was the southernmost area of call for English raiders, an Anglo explorer once noted rice to be so plentiful there as to bring almost no price (Grant 1968: 24-25; Parrish 1942 : 227n.).

The most significant rice region, however, was the "Windward Coast," the area upwind or westward from the major Gold Coast trading station of Elmina. An Englishman who spent time in Sierra Leone on the Windward Coast at the end of the eighteenth century claimed that rice "forms the chief part of the African's sustenance." He went on to observe, "The rice-fields or lugars are prepared during the dry season, and the seed sown in the tornado season, requiring about four or five months growth to bring it to perfection" (Corry 1968 [1807] : 37; cf. Fyfe 1964: 20, 29, 77). Throughout the era of forced emigration into South Carolina references can be found concerning African familiarity with rice. Ads in the local papers occasionally made note of Africans from rice-growing areas (Donnan, I: 375, 377-380, 413, 428, 438, 442. See also Mannix and Cowley 1962, opp. 146), and a notice from the *Evening Gazette*, July 11, 1785, announced the arrival aboard a Danish ship of "a choice cargo of [Africans from the] wind-ward and gold coast [region] who have been accustomed to the planting of rice."[10]

Those Africans who were accustomed to growing rice on one side of the Atlantic, and who found themselves raising the same crop on the other side, did not markedly alter their annual routine. When New World Africans planted rice in the spring by pressing a hole with the heel and covering the seeds with the foot, the motion used was demonstrably similar to that employed in West Africa (Herskovits 1937: opp. 100; Bascom 1941: 49). In summer, when Carolina Africans moved through the rice fields in a row, hoeing in unison to work songs, the pattern of cultivation was not one imposed by European owners but rather one retained from West African forebears (Bascom 1941: 45; Glassie 1968: 117). And in October, when the threshed grain was "fanned" in the wind, the wide flat winnowing baskets were made by black hands after an African design (Huggins, Kilson, Fox 1971: opp. 128; Heskovits 1958: 147).

Those familiar with growing and harvesting rice must also have known how to process it, so it is interesting to speculate about the origins of the mortar and pestle technique which became the accepted method for removing rice grains from their husks. Efforts by Europeans to develop alternative "engines" proved of no avail, and this process remained the most efficient way to "clean" the rice crop throughout the colonial period. Since some form of the mortar and pestle is familiar to agricultural peoples throughout the world, a variety of possible (and impossible) sources have been suggested for this device (Glassie 1968: 116-117). But the most logical origin for this technique is the coast of Africa, for there was a strikingly close resemblance between the traditional West African means of pounding rice and the process used by Africans in South Carolina. Several Africans, usually women, cleaned the grain a small amount at a time by putting it in a wooden mortar which was hollowed from the upright trunk of a pine or cypress. It was beaten with long wooden pestles which had a sharp edge at one end for removing the husks and a flat tip at the other for whitening the grains. Even the songs sung by the captured Africans who threshed and pounded the rice may have retained African elements (Herskovits 1958: 147; Parrish 1942: 13, 225-233, plates 7 and 8).

In the establishment of rice cultivation, as in numerous other areas, historians have ignored the possibility that Afro-Americans could have contributed anything more than menial labor to South

Carolina's early development. Yet captured Africans, faced with limited food supplies before 1700 and encouraged to raise their own subsistence, could readily have succeeded in nurturing rice where their masters had failed. It would not have taken many such incidents to demonstrate to the anxious English that rice was a potential staple and that Africans were its most logical cultivators and processors. Some such chain of events may even have provided the background for Edward Randolph's report to the Lords of Trade in 1700 that Englishmen in Carolina had "now found out the true way of raising and husking Rice" (BPRO Trans, IV, 189-190). Needless to say, by no means every forced African immigrant entering South Carolina had been drawn from an African rice field, and many, perhaps even a great majority, had never seen a rice plant. But it is important to consider the fact that literally hundreds of enslaved Africans were more familiar with the planting, hoeing, processing, and cooking of rice than were the European settlers who purchased them.

Despite the usefulness of all such African skills to the colony's development, there existed a reverse side to the coin. While it is clear that African South Carolinians made early contributions to the regional culture, it is also clear that they received little recompense for their participation and that they were bound to respond to this fact. Africans quickly proved that the same abilities which benefited Europeans, such as gathering herbs and guiding canoes, could also be used to oppose and threaten them. The connection between African expertise and African resistance, suggested by the story of Harry's skill in protecting a fort against Anglo-Carolinian soldiers, can be illustrated in a number of areas.

The raising of livestock provides a case in point. As cattle and hog production grew, it provided numerous Anglo-Carolinians with the substance for increasing their holdings of captured Africans (Salley 1911: 172), and European observers marvelled at this growth (Nairne 1710: 13). Africans, on the other hand benefited little from this enterprise in which they were involved. Consequently they began to utilize their skills to the disadvantage of the colonists' society. Africans often helped themselves to the livestock which they tended, and the regulations for branding stock which were introduced by the government before 1700 did little to deter this practice. Africans altered brands with such dexterity that in the Negro Act of 1722 Anglo-Carolinians denied them the right to keep and breed any horses, cow, or hogs whatsoever (*Statutes* II, 106; VII, 382). Nevertheless, livestock rustling by Africans continued, and in 1743 the Assembly was obliged to draft "An Act to prevent Stealing of Horses and Neat Cattle," which went so far as to declare, "it shall not be lawfull hereafter for any [African] whatsoever to brand or mark any horses or neat Cattle but in the Presence of some [Anglo-Carolinian and/or colonist] Person under the penalty of being severely whip[p]ed" (*Statutes* III, 604; cf. IV, 285 (1768).

A law passed the following year required that African ferrymen, suspected of transporting fellow Africans, were to be accompanied by a freeman at all times (*Statutes* III, 626; ix, 72. 1731). By then it had been apparent for decades that the skills of African boatmen could be a liability as well as source of profit to white colonists. As early as 1696 an act had been passed, patterned on laws already in force in the West Indies, which threatened any African who "shall take away or let loose any boat or canoe" with thirty-nine lashes for the first offense and loss of an ear for repetition (*Statutes* II, 105. See Higham for a similar law on Antigua). Related acts in the eighteenth century prohibited unfree Africans from owning or using any boat or canoe without authorization (*Statutes* VII, 368 (1714), 382 (1722), 409-410 (1740)). Such repeated legislation underscores the fact that Africans who were involved in building and manning these boats inevitably found occasions to use them for travel or escape.

Among the Africans whose seamanship was most valuable and also most problematical for whites were those who served aboard Charleston pilot boats or were otherwise knowledgeable in local navigation. The possibility that Africans would make such strategic skills available to an international rival was always a source of concern for English settlers. There was alarm, for example, during hostilities with Spain in 1741 when the Africans from Thomas Poole's pilot boat were carried to St. Augustine by a Spanish privateer (*Journal of the Commons House of Assembly*, 1741-1742, 272). At that time colonists were well aware that for several decades Bermuda had suffered serious depradations from Spanish vessels piloted by Bermuda Africans who had defected (Wilkinson 1950: 112; cf. Wood 350). Four years later an African named Arrah was seized from Hugh Cartwright's schooner and "great encouragement was offered to be given him by the enemy if he would join with them against the English, and assist them as a pilot for... Carolina." When he stoutly refused and succeeded in making his way back to Charleston after several years, the grateful Assembly granted him his freedom by a special act (*Statutes* VII, 419-420).

African knowledge of herbs and poisons was the most vivid reminder that African expertise could be a two-edged sword. In West Africa, the obeah-men and others with the herbal know-how to combat poisoning could inflict it as well, and this gave Africans a weapon against the Anglo-American colonists. In South Carolina the administering of poison by an African was made a felony in the stiff Negro Act of 1740 which followed in the wake of the Stono Rebellion (*Statutes* VII, 402). Eleven years later an additional law was written, stating that "the detestable crime of poisoning hath of late been frequently committed by many slaves in this Province, and notwithstanding the execution of several criminals for that offence, yet it has not been sufficient to deter others from being guilty of the same" (*Statutes* VII, 422-423)...

Alexander Garden (the Charleston physician after whom Linnaeus named the gardenia)... took most seriously the implications that black proficiency derived from Africa. He requested from Alston, "assistance in giving me what information you could about the African Poisons, as I greatly and do still suspect that the [Africans] bring their knowledge of the poisonous plants, which they use here, with them from their own country." He even went so far as to state explicitly that it was part of his plan, "To investigate the nature of particular poisons (chiefly those indigenous in this province and Africa)." But his scheme was of little avail at a time when European knowledge of Africa flora was still so limited.

Europeans entering South Carolina did not anticipate African skills or the uses to which they might be put. Indeed, most were ignorant of the environment they entered and of the labor they purchased. But Anglo-Carolinian settlers soon realized that African workers possessed expertise which could be exploited and knowledge which was to be feared. Within several generations, the Europeans had imparted aspects of their culture to the Africans and had themselves acquired practical knowledge in matters such as rice growing (Corry 1968 [1807], 65-66). Consequently, African skills rapidly lost distinctiveness during the middle decades of the eighteenth century...*

---

* However, it was those skills, the geo-political regional advantages, the rivalries between the different colonial powers (including England), etc., that set the stage for the U.S.' most bloody civil war against enslavement and occupation by the African and Indian Seminoles. It was the social and geo-political position of the Africans in South Carolina that made this war possible, a war that all efforts were made to rewrite, downplay, and render invisible.

ENDNOTES

1   Landgrave Thomas Smith, Dr. Henry Woodward, an anonymous sea captain, and a treasurer of the East Indian Company all took or received the credit at some point. A letter of Nov. 4, 1726 (overlooked by historians), from Jean Watt in Neufchatel makes the claim "that it was by a woman that Rice was transplanted into Carolina." Records of the British Public Record Office Relating to South Carolina (hereafter abbreviated as BPRO Trans.), xii, 156-157.

2   At the end of the eighteenth century the Abbe Raynal wrote: "Opinions differ about the manner in which rice hath been naturalized in Carolina. But whether the province may have acquired it by a shipwreck, or whether it may have been carried there with Africans, or whether it be sent from England, it is certain that the soil is favourable for it" (Raynal, London, 1798, VI, 59).
     The first edition of this work, in 1772. offered only the shipwreck theory. The tradition of a Madagascar origin has been popularized in Heyward 1937. On slaves from that region, see Platt 1969: 548-577.

3   A copy of this letter (Jan. 10, 1726) is in volume II (labelled volume III) of the typescript marked, "Charleston Museum, Miscellaneous Papers, 1726-1730," South Caroliniana Library, Columbia.

4   It is impossible to say whether it was Africans or Indians who showed white planters, around 1700, how to put a gourd on a pole as a birdhouse for martins (that would in turn drive crows from the crops) or who fashioned the first drinking gourd which would become the standard dipper on plantations.

5   In 1682 Thomas Newe found that horses brought from New England were still scarce and expensive, "so there is but little use of them, all Plantations being seated on the Rivers, they can go to and fro by Canoo or Boat as well and as soon as they can ride." Newe added that "the horses here like the Indians and many of the English do travail without shoes" (Salley 1911 : 184).

6   The English experience in Carolina must have been comparable to that of the French among the Island Caribs of the Antilles at the same time. Breton (1665, reprinted 1892), 331 states:
          The French learned from the Savages to hollow out
          trees to make canoes; but they did not learn from them
          to row them, steer them, or jump overboard to right
          them when they overturned" the Savages are not afraid
          of overturning, wetting their clothes, losing anything,
          or drowning, but most French fear all of these things…
          Every day one sees disastrous accidents.

7   Frederic G. Cassidy (1967) points out that the Doulla-Bakweri language of the Cameroon River area provided the Jamaican Creole word for the crayfish or river prawn. "This part of Africa, indeed, took its name from the plentiful shrimp or prawns in the river: Cameroon is from Portuguese camarao 'shrimp.'"

8   In 1673, for example, Edmund Lister of Northumberland County, Virginia, bought one hundred acres of land along the Ashley river on Oyster Point from an illiterate laborer named John Gardner. Lister sent three men south ahead of him to prepare the land (not an unusual practice), but he died the following year before taking up residence. One of those he had sent ahead to South Carolina was an indenture servant named Patrick Steward with only several months left to serve, but the others were apparently black slaves experienced with livestock, for

in 1676 Lister's widow stated in a bill of sale that her "Decd housband, did formerly Transport Severall Negros, out of this Colony of Virginia, into Carolina and did there Settle them upon a Plantacon, together wtd Some Cattle." The holding may have been considerable, for the widow received 10.000 pounds of good tobacco for the land, Negroes, and stock from a Virginia gentleman who was himself an absentee owner of slave in Carolina (South Carolina Archives, Records of the Secretary of the Province, 1675-1695, 39-41 ; Salley 1944 (1671-1675) : 59, 66-69). It was long ago suggested that the particularly numerous slaves in the Narragansett country of Rhode Island played an important role on the renowned stock farms of that region (Channing 1886: 9-10).

[9] A letter from the Reverend John Urmstone in North Carolina, July 11, 1711 (quoted in Land 22-23), typifies conditions which had prevailed in South Carolina slightly earlier. Urmstone stated, "the planter here is but a slave to raise a provision for other colonies," adding:

Men are generally of all trades, and women the like within their spheres, except some who are the posterity of old planters, and have great number of slaves, who understand most handicraft......

[10] The most dramatic evidence of experience with rice among enslaved Africans comes from the famous rebels aboard the Amistad in the nineteenth century. Thirty-six Africans from the Sierra Leone region were shipped illegally from Lomboko to Cuba, and in the wake of their successful shipboard uprising they eventually found themselves imprisoned in New Haven. There they were interrogated separately, and excerpts from the interviews drive home this familiarity with rice in personal terms:

He was a blacksmith in his native village, and made hoes, axes and knives; he also planted rice. There are high mountains in his country, rice is cultivated, people have guns has seen elephants. He was caught in the bush by four men as he was going to plant rice; his left hand was tied to his neck; was ten days going to Lomboko.
He was seized by four men when in a rice field, and was two weeks in travelling to Lomboko
He is a planter of rice.
His parents are dead, and he lived with his brother, a planter of rice.
He was seized by two men as he was going to plant rice.
5 ft. 1 in. high, body tatto4ed, teeth filed, was born at Fe-baw, in Sando, between Mendi and Konno. His mother's brother sold him for a coat. He was taken in the night, and sold to Garloba, who had four wives. He staid with this man two years, and was employed in cultivating rice. His master's wives and children were employed in the same manner, and no distinction made in regard to labor (Barber 1969 (1840): 9-15).

BIBLIOGRAPHY

1775   American Husbandry. London. (Reprinted in Aubrey C. Land).
Aptheker, Herbert.
        1969   *American Negro Slave Revolts*. 2nd. Ed. New York.
Baker, H.G.
        1962   "Comments on the thesis that there was a major centre of plant domestication near the headwaters of the River Niger". Journal of African History 3: 229-234.

Barber, John Warner
    1840 *A History of the Amistad Captives.* New Haven. (Reprinted New York, 1969).
Barnwell, J.
    1898 *Virginia Magazine of History and Biography,* VI (July): 44-45.
Bascom, William R.
    1941 "Acculturation among the Gullah Negroes". *American Anthropologist* XLIII: 43-50.
Batutah, Ibn (Muhammed ibn abd Allah).
    1929 *Travels in Asia and Africa, 1325-1354.* Translated and selected by H.A.R. Gibb. London.
Boshchi, Charles
    1949 To S.P.G. Secretary, Oct. 20, 1745. *South Carolina Historical and Geneological Magazine* L (October): 185.
Breton R.P. Raymond
    1892 *Dictionnaire Caraibe-Francais, 1665.* (Reprinted Leipzig 1892.)
Brickell, John
    1737 *The Natural History of North-Carolina.* London. (Reprinted, Raleigh, 1911).
Burton, E. Milby
    1955 *Charleston Furniture, 1700-1825.* Charleston.
Cassidy, Frederic G.
    1967 "Some New Light on Old Jamaicanisms". *American Speech* XLII: 191-192.
Catesby, Mark
    1743 *The Natural History of Carolina, Florida and the Bahama Islands.* London.
Channing, Edward
    1886 "The Narragansett Planters". Johns Hopkins University Studies in Historical and Political Science, Series 4, No. 3. Baltimore.
Clark, J.D.
    1962 "The spread of food production in Sub-Saharan Africa". *Journal of African History* 3: 211-228.
Clontes, F.W.
    1926 "Travel and Transportation in Colonial North Carolina". *North Carolina Historical Review* III (January): 16-35.
Clowse, Converse D.
    1971 *Economic Beginnings in Colonial South Carolina, 1670-1730.* Columbia.
Conner, Jeanette Thurber, trans. and ed.
    1930 *Colonial records of Spanish Florida* III (June 4, 1580). Deland, Florida.
Cooper, Thomas and David J. McCord, eds.
    1836-1841 *The Statutes at Large of South Carolina.* 10 vols. Columbia.
Corry, Joseph
    1807 *Observations upon the Windward Coast of Africa.* London. (Reprinted, London, 1968).
Crum, Mason
    1940 *Gullah: Negro Life in the Carolina Sea Islands.* Durham, North Carolina.
Curtin, Philip D.
    1968 "Epidemiology and the slave trade". *Political Science Quarterly* LXXXIII (June): 119-216.

106

Donnan, Elizabeth, ed.
    1930-1935   *Documents Illustrative of the Slave Trade to America.*
    Whasington.
Dunbar, Gary S.
    1961   "Colonial Carolina Cowpens". *Agricultural History* XXXV: 125-
    130.
Duncan, John D.
    1972   "Slave emancipation in colonial South Carolina". *American
    Chronical, A. Magazine of History* I (January): 64-66.
Dundes, Alan
    1965   "African Tales among the North American Indians". *Southern
    Folklore Quarterly* 29 (September): 207-219.
Fisher, Miles Mark
    1953   *Negro slave songs in the United States.* New York.
Fyfe, Christopher
    1964   *Sierra Leone inheritance.* London.
Glassie, Henry
    1968   "Patterns in the Material Folk Culture of the Eastern United
    States". University of Pennsylvania Monographs. In Folklore
    and Folklife, No. 1. Philadelphia.
Glenn James
    1761   *A Description of South Carolina.* London. (Reprinted in
    Chapman J. Milling, ed., *Colonial South Carolina: Two
    Contemporary descriptions.* Columbia, 1951).
Grant, Douglas
    1968   *The Fortunate Slave, An Illustration of African Slavery in the
    Early Eighteenth Century.* London.
Gray, Lewis Cecil
    1933   *History of Agriculture in the Southern United States to 1860.*
    Washington.
Hakluyt, Ricahrd
    1904   *The Principal Navigations, Voyages, Traffiques & Disoveries
    of the English Nation*, X. Glasgow.
Heskovits, Melville J.
    1930   "The culture areas of Africa". Africa III" 67-73.
    1937   *Life in a Haititan Valley.* New York.
    1941   *The Myth of the Negro Past.* Boston.
Heyward, Duncan Clinch
    1937   *Seed from Madagascar.* Chapel Hill.
Higham, C.S.S.
    1921   *The Development of the Leeward Islands, 1660-1688.*
    Cambridge, England.
Hudson, Charles M., ed.
    1971   "Red, White, and Black, Symposium on Indians in the Old South."
    Southern Anthropological Society, Proceedings, No. 5. Athens,
    Georgia.
Huggins, Nathan I., Martin Kilson, Daniel M. Fox, eds.
    1971   *Key Issues in the Afro-American Experience.* New York.
Journal of the Commons House of Assembly, 1726-1727.
Land, Aubrey C.
    1969   *Bases of the Plantation Society.* Columbia.
Lawson, John.

1709　*A New Voyage to Carolina.* London. (Republished with introduction and notes by Hugh Talmage Lefler, Chapel Hill, 1967).

Levi-Strauss, Claude
1966　T*he Savage Mind.* London.

McCall, Daniel F.
1964　*Africa in Time-Perspective.* Boston.

McCrady, Edward
1899　*The History of South Carolina Under the Royal Government, 1719-1776.* New York.

McKusick, Marshall B.
1960　"Aboriginal canoes in the West Indies", in Sidney W. Mintz (comp.), *Papers in Caribbean Anthropology.* Yale university Publications in Anthropology, No. 57. New Haven.

McPherson, et al., eds.
1971　"African cultural survivals among Black Americans", in *Blacks in America: Bibiographical Essays.* Garden City.

Mannix, Daniel P. and Malcolm Cowley.
1962　Black Cargoes: A History of the Atlantic Slave Trade, 1518-1865. New York.

Marburg, H. and W.H. Crawford.
1802　*Digest of the Laws of Georgia.* Savannah.

Mathews, Mitford
1938-1944　*A Dictionary of American English.* Chicago.

Montlzun, Baron de
1948　"A Frenchman Visits Charleston, 1817." *South Carolina Historical and Genealogical Magazine* XLIX (July) : 136.

Morgan W. B.
1962　"The forest and agriculture in West Africa". *Journal of African History* 3: 235-240.

Mullin, Gerald W.
1972　*Flight and Rebellion: Slave Resistance in Eighteenth-Century Virginia.* New York.

Naire, Thomas
1710　A Letter from South Carolina. London.

Parrish, Lydia
1942　*Slave Songs of the Georgia Sea Islands.* New York.

Patterson, Orlando
1967　*The Sociology of Slavery, An Analysis of the Origins, Development and Structure of Negro Society in Jamaica.* London.

Pemberton, James, *Diary of a trip to South Carolina, 1745,* entry for October 17, original in Library of Congress, mfm. In South Caroliniana Library, Columbia.

Platt, Virginia Bever
1969　"The East India Company and the Madagascar slave trade". *William and Mary Quarterly,* 3rd ser., XXVI (October): 548-577.

Price, Richard.
1968　"Caribbean fishing and fishermen: a historical sketch". *American Anthropologist* LXVIII: 1363-1383.

Quigley, Carroll
1956　"Aboriginal fish poisons and the diffusion problem". *American Anthropologist* LVIII: 508-525.

Raynal, Abbe

1798   *Philosophical and Political History of the Possessions and Trade of Europeans in the Two Indies*. 2nd. Ed. London.
Records of the British Public Record Office Relating to South Carolina, 36 vols. (1663-1782). (In the South Carolina Department of Archives and History).
Salley, Alexander S., ed.
    1911   *Narratives of Early Carolina, 1650-1708*. New York.
    1919   "The Introduction of Rice Culture into South Carolina" (Bulletins of the Historical Commission of South Carolina, No. 6). Columbia.
    1944   *Records* of the Secretary of the Province and the Register of the Province of South Carolina, 1671-1675. Columbia.
Schaw, Janet
    1922   *Journal of a Lady of Quality*, edited by Evangeline W. Andrews and Charles M. Andrews. New Haven.
Smith, Alice R. Huger
    1936   *A Carolina Rice Plantation of the Fifties*. New York.
South Carolina Historical Society, Collections, in the South Carolina Department of Archives and History.
Sutherland, James
    Undated letter in the Coe Papers (Documents of the Lords Commissioners, 1719-1742). South Carolina Historical Society.
Thibou, Louis
    Letter in French dated September 20, 1683 and typescript translation in the South Carolina Library, Columbia.
Turberville, A.S.
    1929   *English Men and Manners in the Eighteenth Century*. 2nd ed. London.
Vensina, Jan
    1971   "Once upon a time: oral traditions as history in Africa". *Daedalus* C (Spring): 442-468.
Waring, Joseph I.
    1964   *A history of Medicine in South Carolina, 1670-1825*. Charleston.
Wax, Darold D.
    1968   "A Philadelphia surgeon on a slaving voyage to Africa, 1749-1751". *Pennsylvania Magazine of History and Biography* XCII (October): 474-478.
Webber, Mabel L., comp.
    1914   "South Carolina Almanacs, to 1800". *South Carolina Historical and Genealogical Magaxine* XV (April): 78.
Weston, P. C. J., ed.
    1856   Documents Connected with the History of South Carolina. London.
Whitten, Norman E., Jr., and John F. Szwed
    1970   *Afro-American Anthropology" Contemporary Perspectives*. New York.
Wilkindson, Henry C.
    1950   *Bermuda in the Old Empire*. London.
Wills, Inventories and Miscellaneous Records, in the South Carolina Department of Archives and History.
Wood, Peter H.
    1972   "Black majority: Negroes in colonial South Carolina from 1670 through the Stono Rebellion". Ph. D. dissertation, Harvard University.

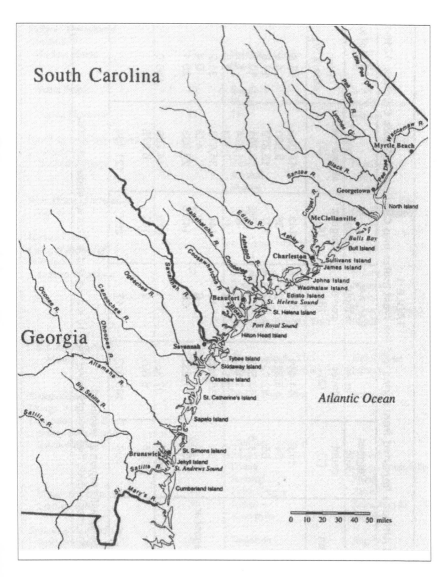

Coastal Area of South Carolina and Georgia
where the Gullah-Geechee culture first evolved through the
interactions of forcibly immigrated Africans who spoke diverse
languages and came from diverse African cultures. "[T]here they
greatly outnumbered whites, preserving their biological integrity
and molding their distinctive patterns of language and culture."
William S. Pollitzer, *Historical Methods*, Spring 1993, Vol. 25, No. 2.

CHAPTER FOUR

THE HIDDEN MUSLIM PRESENCE IN EARLY AFRICAN AMERICAN HISTORY

An Oral History of the First Muslim Community in the U.S.

from Gullah-Geechee Elder
CORNELIA BAILEY
on her great-great-great-grandfather,
BILALI
Interview by Elder Carlie Towne
in the company of Elder Halim Gullahbeme
and Elder Lisa Wineglass Smalls

CT: Talk about the life of Bilali's family in Africa before he arrived in the New World.

C: Now, I read that and I said to myself, Okay, what do I know about my great-great-great grandfather before he came here. Some cousin we talked about who works at the paper—she went over a couple of times, I think two or three times, trying to find him and his ancestry. Even before that, we were trying to find the pieces and saying, there's a lot of conjecture about what he might have been doing down there. Was he actually born in that area? Or was he a student in that area? So most people surmise that he was a student in that area, not actually born in that area, because his facial features didn't put him among the Africans in that particular area. Their facial feature came from Egypt or some place, and so he came from a little further away than there. And being a student of the Islamic faith, he probably

CORNELIA BAILEY
Gullah Elder

happen to be in the wrong place at the wrong time when the slavers came through. And he end up in this part over here. Cause, they then firmly believe that he was not from there.

CT: But there is some research that is being done…
C: There is some research being done, we're looking. We found out that there's the elders of the community, the keepers of the scrolls in that community. And they say it's very hard for you to get them to release the scrolls. It seems like there's hidden information there that we need about him and that we found out: that he could read and write. Then the next question is, when he got captured there, was he already a full-grown man or was he a teenager? And he went from there to the West Indies, and then from there to Sapelo. So. how long did he stay in any one of these places? We have just as much questions as he have. It's like how long did he stay in the Bahamas? Was his wife from that area? We know pretty well that he brought his wife from there to here...

CT: So, he actually went to the Bahamas?

C: Yeah, as a slave. They bought him from Africa to the Bahamas. And from the Bahamas to here.

CT: So, his wife was actually from the Bahamas?

C: From what we think…from the Bahamas. Yeah. There he acquired his wife—from there. The records show that when he came to Sapelo he already had his wife and children. So, he at least had them when he was there. Now, we don't know if he had them when he was there [in Africa] but then, see, those are some of the contradictions. Because, then, also, one of his great granddaughters saying that her great grandmother told them of the kind of house that they lived in in Africa. So, once again, you looking at what she's saying. And oral history among Blacks is very important, [more] than what the white man eventually end up writing own. Because there are more conjections than yours, because yours are more word of mouth. And word of mouth even today is still good. And she described the type of house that they lived in in Africa. The thatched roof and the type of animals that was there. And so…obviously one of those daughters was born in Africa and not in the Bahamas. And so…so, it still bears a lot more research.

_____

* Dr. Y. N. Kly, who requested the interview be conducted

CT: Okay. Well, that's good. At least we know that you've gotten this much information and you're still looking into it.

C: Yes. Mmm Hmm. So, I don't know if he's* got copies of *Drums and Shadows* or not, but tell him he needs to get a copy of *Drums and Shadows* 'cause, Katie Brown, one of his granddaughters, talked about what her grandmother told her and so forth about him…

CT: Okay. That's really, really interesting.. Then he wants to know, what school of Islam did he follow?

C: Now, I'm not that proficient in it…we had some students who's trying to figure out which one he might have…because when his writing first surfaced, whites thought it was him keeping in a native handwriting, a record of the plantation. And later there was some students who were proficient in 'Old Arabic', they call it…Ancient Arabic. And so, he was writing Ancient Arabic, not the Arabic of today as we know it. And so, they transcribed it to the fact that he was actually talking about the rules and regulations to follow, being a good, Muslim. And then, in his old age—they were not allowed to write while they was a slave—and was too old to work, they figure then he decided to put down what he remembered from being in school.

CT: That is…?

C: And the deciphering part…The part that the ink didn't completely fade out what you could read. And they deciphered it for us an' translated it for us, so it was interesting because I'm reading this translated thing, I'm going, "We did that…We *do* that!" …It was actually, it was interesting to see. I'm going, "Wait a minute here, you know?!" (Laughter). Yeah. The similarities was great.

CT: Yeah. So, you actually have copies of those?

C: Yeah. They have it in the archives in Atlanta…but you have copies of 'em. I have to dig 'em but I have copies around here, too. Somebody gave me copies of 'em… Imagine, I actually touched it! The diary that he wrote…because, they had it at display…and so, being the great-great-great-granddaughter of Bilali, they take it from under the lock and keys.

CT: Oh, that's wonderful.

C: So, I actually handled it…Couldn't understand it, but I actually handled it! (Laughter). Just to handle it was good enough, you know?!

CT: I know! I know! That's just putting you back in history.

C: Yeah and it was like, "Wow! My great-great-great-great…yeah… on my Mother's side. Yeah.

CT: How was he captured? Does anybody know that?

C: Well, not particularly. You know, capture was kind of a particular thing…And…and people don't know exactly how one group was captured. But, I can tell you one thing, in our society on sapelo, we hated red.

CT: Hated red?

C: Red. R-e-d. Color red.

CT: Why?

C: Because they say the color red was what helped capture a lot of us and brought us out of he country. 'Cause you know, as in most African fabric, you would see the color red is not in it. So, red was like, uh,…you know people say, well now, a red flag is a warning. You know, people, red flag now goes up. And it's passed down. My mother, my grandmother…all of them, they hated the color red because they said, they—they—slavers, when they came over to capture slaves, they brought 'em with something that they never seen. Which was red…the color red. Red material. And were fascinated by it. And so a lot of us got captured by the color red. And they hated red. And…and…the older people still today, you see 'em, some of em', would never wear red (Laughter) 'Cause it's passed down.

CT: Isn't that something?

C: They hate wearing red…yeah..so….

CT: That's some information for all of us tonight.

C: 'Cause red was a tricky color! So, then, later, red got evolved into a round to the thing that if a woman wear red then you know she was a harlot.

CT: A loose woman

C: ...and a loose woman

CT: Yes! Yes!

C: Because it was tricky and so the red was for tricking people. And henceforth, the red...you know...A woman wearing red, well, she's supposed to have a bag of tricks, too! (Laughter).

CT: Oh, gee.

C: Red was it. Yeah, man...They didn't have nothing to do with red. So, we don't know if he enticed by the color red. Or whether he was a warring tribe and he could've gotten captured in one of those. A lot of times when they warring among themselves, you know, they also got captured and sold off. As slaves to the British and others who were dealing in the slave trade and so forth. So, yeah, so, we never had a clear understanding how...how he got captured. But he end up...he end up in the West Indies in the Bahamas...

CT: That's really so...what can I say? Fascinating!

C: Yes, they hated red. They would say, take that red off. That's hot...how come a lot of us got here in the first place. Hated red. (Laughter). Yes. So, so...any place in your psyche as you get to thinking about it and you listen to some of the older people...you'll remember red.

CT: I remember... I remember. We had, I think, they painted different colors you know, for different things and I think red for us was, you painted the door red to repel the devil. I think it was.

C: Yeah, cause that was a temptation. You know, red (laughter) So, really hated red.

CT: What was the situation in the New World when Bilali got here? Do you have any information on that? When he got where he was going...What was the situation there?

C: Thomas Balding was the one that suppose purchased him from the Bahamas. So, he was purchase by Thomas Balding in the Bahamas and they say that he was such an astute businessman—is how they put it—hat he was able to wrangle a deal for the whole entire family. Very seldom, you know, they always split slave families up. But he ended up on Sapelo with his whole entire family. Grown children, near grown children..So, that's how come we're all here, because of his kids. His daughters….We don't know too much about his sons. We think the sons eventually start using the name 'Smith', but we can trace his daughters a lot quicker. 'Cause, you know, in the black society, white man put it so where we got traced through our Mothers instead of Fathers. So they can deny ownership… So, the Mother was the way the gene pool went. Through the Mother. So he had seven daughters and we're the product of one of his seven daughters.

CT: Oh…we've just got to keep on going!

C: (Laughter) so, we're the seven…matter of fact we even got a rose that we call the Seven Sisters Rose of Sapelo…. there is a seven sisters rose other places, but we connect with our history of the Seven Sisters and the Seven Daughters. So, the Seven Sister Rose, Seven daughters, which is Seven Sisters.

CT: What language did Bilali speak?

C: He spoke English and he spoke Arabic. Now, what form of Arabic, because I'm not astute in Arabic….but he spoke Arabic among his family and among….there was a couple of other people on the island at that time also who were Arabic speakers who was Muslims. So, the ones who was Muslims spoke Arabic among themselves because his grandchildren all…they all report that when they're among themselves they speak a language that they couldn't understand.

CT: True.

C: Yeah…so they spoke Arabic. So, he wasn't the only Muslim-speaking guy here. There were others…in this area. There's a few others on Sapelo and there's on the mainland and other places and they were others as well. But, uh, they were very few of 'em. So, uh, there wasn't that many.

CT: Well, you already answered the question, did he write, because you said he was such an astute businessman and he got his whole family. So, I know he wrote.

C: Yeah. And so he wrote…or he can bargain like heck! I'll tell you that. Yes…so, he had to be a very likeable person to do that…. And my Grandmother…Grandmama used to always tell us, say, "You know, the rest of the black people…in her generation, even her, she say…. you know, the rest of the colored people here didn't like our people. We were one of them, but she say, you know…you know…they never really liked us…because we were different."

CT: Different, huh?

C: Yeah.

CT: When she said different…what did she…

C: Well, she was talking about the religion and the belief and other stuff that we were different and that we also kept more to ourself. We kinda…a lot of old people would say, "We held ourselves… in a certain way". So, we was a little bit different, they really didn't like us for that. Grandmama say, they never really like us…(laughter) and then, plus that, Grandpa was the overseer. And a overseer, whether you black or white, you gotta be kinda tough. So, you could imagine…he wasn't very well liked. (Laughter). Also, here he was, this man with a different religion, can speak a different tongue and also the white boss at the time appointed him over all the rest of 'em…so, you could see…he wasn't very liked.

CT: So, in other words then, Arabic was actually his native tongue

C: That was…must be…his native tongue. So, that's another reason why they think that he was not born in that particular part of Africa near the Niger River. Uh, they think he was…he was just there…because that was not the native tongue of the people there.

CT: Does any of his writings, we talked about the Arabic that he did that we can probably find in the archives. But, did he do any other writings that we can find?

C: Not that we know of. Because, see, that particular piece of work of his was… he left the island for a short space of time and went.. We don't know how this white minister…Presbyterian minister, I think, got ahold to his writing. I don't know if he befriended him and,

GULLAH ELDER LISA WINEGLASS SMALLS

GULLAH ELDERS HALIM GULLAHBEMI AND CARLIE TOWNE

in his old age or what, but... he ended up wit it. And later he ended up turning it over to, I think, the University of Georgia system or something. So, if he left anything else with him, the guy probably thought it wasn't anything of importance, except, he thought that one was important and he kept that ...yeah.

CT: Do you know what year the majority of people in Sophia and Durian were Muslim?

C: There never was a majority of Muslim. And still isn't ...and the reason for that is, even in religion we was, we were controlled by the white man. And the white man did not recognize the Islamic faith. And so you were forbidden to practice it. So the people that practiced the Islamic faith did it in secret.

CT: O.K.

C: So it was never a majority. So you would fool sometime, so you didn't want to get all people nerved. They say "What religion are you?" I say, "Born Muslim and became forced Christian" so that confused the heck out of them.

CT: Yeah. (Laughter.)

C: And they look at me. Huh?? And I say, "You heard what I said."

CT: Mm hum. (Laughter.)

C: And so as black people, as black people, especially we was taught we didn't have any kind of religious background. Except Voodooism and so forth. So we hadn't any formal religious background. And so when I went to Africa first time, went to this archives and this museum. And the curator carry us through, had this three objects on table. And he say this is the holy—the three basic religions, the three major religions of the world. Here's the Holy Bible, here's the Quran and here's a rock to represent the other. And I stood there and looked at that, as everybody else move and going to something else. And I say, why is he saying that ... and I would have had the rock first. This is my country, I would have said. The rock would have been first, the Quran would have been second and the Holy Bible third. I would have been true to the faith because Muslim religion came there before Christianity. So I would have had it in that order instead of the other order, and I stood there for the longest duration thinking, ' Why did he do that?'

C: And so we sometimes I think that we are people that straddling the fence in a lot of ways. We straddling the fence, we go to church, we are the Baptist, or we're the Jehovah Witness, or we're Episcopalians. But there is still something missing, no matter what. No matter how the Preacher's preaching, or the choir sing, there is something missing, as if we are not complete. As if we are leaving a part of something out. We are never completely satisfied. I tell people that—don't get me wrong, I believe in God, but there is something missing in the teaching that has not reached a majority of Black people so that they can settle down and say: this is it. So we are still wondering out there.

CT: In May, I was talking earlier to Elder Helena, Elder Elisa, and whatever we really are comes out. We don't know why, but you know why, because you know the history

C: And we are forever searching. We are still searching. We are still wandering like the wanderers of the desert, we are still searching. And we go switching, we have people who have this religion all their life and all of a sudden they change and they don't change the church down the street, they change the whole different thing altogether because we are still searching.

CT: True

C: The white Catholic, and most of the Catholic stay Catholic no matter what they do. But we don't, and so if something is missing we will change, and so we are still looking for something.

CT: Well you seem to have a lot of the links that we, that a lot of people are looking for.

C: But that also leaves me in a peculiar position where people will once again, will think that you are different. (Laughter) Because you dare mention you're different, or you dare live your difference, and they look at you like: what's wrong with her or what's wrong with him and so I'm used to it, so it doesn't bother me. Once I find that I can stand on my own ground or my own two feet and what I think is like, well it doesn't matter. My own thing is: as long as I am not disobeying any law of God and man, to get me in trouble, then the rest of you just leave me alone. (Laughter.)

CT: That's one way of looking.

C: And so it works or else you will be living someone else's life.

CT: I agree with you. Now we got a lot of information today and I'm really excited.

C: You went to the church today and that church was formed by the children and grandchildren of Bilali.

CT: Yes. They talked about that today.

C: I made them do it, because the lady minister—you probably mention my cousin, Caroline Daust—when I first told her, I said Carolina you're a Baptist minister, but let me tell your background is Islamic.

CT: Oh really, what did she say.

C: She stood still for the longest without saying anything. I said, let me give you a bit of your history, here, I said. And your great-great grandfather was Bilali the Muslim. And I said, now who do you think organized the church in 1865, and I said that it was his children and grandchildren and so forth. I said that he ran a strict Muslim household. So that when they built the church, organized the church here, they sit around at a table or someplace and made rules on how the church was going to be operated, and it was part Muslim and part Christianity.

C: So it was split down the middle. We didn't get handed a fellow-ship to become a member. We had to go through a ritual like some of the tribes in Africa still got to go through—a ritual to become something. We had two to three months we had to go before the elders every day, and the elders taught us every day of the ways we had to do, and they would decipher the dreams. The dreams are the things that took you over. We had to decipher your dreams, had to decipher the bible verse that you brought every day. Everything was deciphered and explained for you, and when they decided that you were ready, they would bring you before the other elders, and they would listen to one of your dreams and your teacher explain it to them. Then they say that she's ready...

CT: That she's ready

C: ... or he's ready. Other than that you were turned back, and you had to go out into the wilderness. And you still get tribes in Africa who, when a young man get a certain age, has to go out into the wilderness and has to prove himself by killing an animal or something. We had to go out in the wilderness in the middle of the night. It was called the wilderness. We didn't have to kill an animal, but we had to go out and meditate and pray by ourself for one hour.

CT: Right.

C: Every night. And our family was strict on it. You had to go out there and stay out there for one hour.

CT: For one hour.

C: That's right. Every night by yourself. Nobody knows that secret spot but you. You can play around that spot all day with your friends, but you couldn't tell them that was your secret spot, at all. That was yours. And so you see them write in the book. They said Bilali prayed to the east, to Mecca three times a day. He actually prayed five times a day. They saw him pray three times a day; in the morning at daylight, at twelve o'clock at daylight, in the afternoon at daylight. But they didn't see his night prayer before he went to bed. They didn't see his prayer when he rise early in the morning. So they only saw him pray three times a day. Which is why he pray three to five times. So they only write what they saw.

CT: But that was part of the question, "How did he practice Islam?" Now you say that he had a strict household.

C: Oh, his whole household was strict.

CT: What did they do?

C: They prayed, umm. They all did the same prayer, they prayed all religiously on a prayer rug five times a day, and so forth. There were certain things that they didn't do. Certain people that they didn't mingle with, and way back then, they didn't eat pork. It became after they start evolving that they eat pork, but they didn't eat pork and so forth, and they always prayed.

CT: Mmhum.

C: In our household, when we was growing up, you know kids say prayer, kids had to say prayers, we had to say our prayers, especially our bed time prayer when we had to go to bed. But then you had to be careful how you kneel. You could not, if your bed was situated in your room, get to the front of your bed, kneeling and facing that way—well, don't kneel to your bed. You kneel some place else 'cause God resides on his Throne in the East and the Devil sits on his in the West, so you never, you never bow down. And you see the churches, how the churches, it's designed and built, probably people lost the meaning. You went to the church down there.

CT: Yeah.

C: And you went in the congregation and you were facing the east. Always. Every congregation face east. 'Cause of Mecca. And you go into the cemetery, and your cemetery too, your feet facing east. Your feet is facing this way .So they believe that when Gabriel blow his horn on Judgment morning, you rise up and face God, you're facing that way. So your feet is pointing that way already, and so you stand straight up and face that way. You don't face that way [gesture] so everybody is looking that way, and that is the way they look, you look the way of the rising sun. And so that's the belief, and that was his belief and it was passed down and is still every body's belief.

CT: Wow that is very…

C: Yes, and so when you listen to the old people, they say Maker, when they go to my Maker, they say Mecca. When the old people are saying it fast, they say Mecca.

CT: Ok, that's true.

C: Listen to them carefully, when I'm going to my Mecca, my Maker.

C: And you say, people say, the Islamic word is Salaam. We say, "so long". Over the years it has evolved: so long. I see you tomorrow if God is willing our life lies. We still say it. And so you would be surprised the stuff we say in everyday life. We never stop and think. Over the years we went to school and got educated, and it start changing a bit, whether you start picking apart. You realize that—wait a minute—that's what my great-grandparents were saying, and so forth. And it makes all the difference in the world. It kind of brings pieces back together, and makes you a better person. You know who you are, and so forth, and it's great. Yeah. So that's what I do then, I sit there, go to church and my thing is: I go to church and listen to the minister picking things apart, and in my mind, I going: that's not right, you're suppose to ... (Laughter) maybe as bad as this.

CT: But then, you know, you know that side of you and the truth is there.

C: I'm at the church the other day and the minister said, you all must come to church right, cause one of there days you all gonna be laying in front of an alter someplace on that last day where you'll be buried, and, he said, do something at church and make it worth while because you don't want the minister get up there and lie over you. My head flip up like this and I'm going: now why would you want a minister to lie over you, anyhow? And why would a minister say that in the first place?

CT: That's right.

C: If I didn't do anything, you don't make it up inside in something. And he is saying, don't let the minister stand up there and lie over you and I'm going—well that was the worst thing I ever heard in my life! (Laughter) I look up at him and I look at him straight in the eye and he is probably looking at me and he probably saying, uh oh. (oh no) (Laughter) Gee whiz you don't lie over me.

CT: How did you all bathe for prayers?

C: You had to wash. When I read the transcripts, when they tran-scribe some of his works, when he give the ritual of preparing for prayer, the hand and the face, the top part and the body part, your feet. You know, it was like you got to be kidding. It was so ingrained in us, girl, you wouldn't believe. You couldn't even go to bed with a dirty feet, you wasn't allowed. But if you went to bed with your feet dirty, you had to get out of the bed and wash it and go back into bed. That's how bad it was, you could not. You would toss and turn and until you get out of bed, get that water, wash that feet and go back into bed. And my father he said a man must never wash his back deliberately.

CT: Ok

C: Rub his back. But never wash it. Because a man's strength lie in his back. So he would have us and mom or anybody, he turn his back, give you a rag, wet that rag, no suds in it and have you rub his back in a circular motion until it burns. But never soap in his back. If he got caught in a marine or went swimming that's different thing, But you never deliberately wash your back.

CT: There's so much that a lot of scholars will be very interested in what you have to say.

C: Yeah. Because I refuse to lose the old ways and I ask questions. Boy, I'm on the phone every day saying exactly what did they?(Laughter) Because one day, the older people going, then it's gone. And education is one of the worst things. And I always tell people now don't get me wrong, we need education, but we have gotten so that education replaces everything. It doesn't, it does not replace everything. I said, if you smart enough to send your child off to school, and they come back and they say that they are proficient in five languages—what's wrong, they couldn't keep the old ways, and learn their college studies, and keep the two together? They have to drop the old ways altogether to pick up the new ways? That's not right. We smart enough to master five different languages, we master, we able to live both lives, and keep our tradition and culture. And so I don't think that we should abandon anything.

CT: I agree with that because in abandonment.

C: Abandonment, yeah.

CT: It's like me sitting here now, wanting to know.

C: And later we come back trying to find these things.

CT: Exactly.

C: Trying to find what happened, and who went where, and stuff like that. We should teach our kids, so now, re-teach this generation, ask questions and not to be ashamed of anything. We got a ways to go.

CT: Yeah, we got a ways to go.

C: Yeah.

CT: Because you are the carriers of the culture.

C: So we relearning, we are the bearers of the culture because we have nobody to blame but ourselves.

CT: We talking about Bilali's grave. Where was he buried?

C: Now that is a question. It is reported that he was buried with his Quran and his fez and his prayer book. But now, where? Because we have a cemetery here, we have Behavior Cemetery, which we still uses, but there was another cemetery called Orleans, called New Orleans, and it's abandoned a long time ago before I came around. I think it was abandoned some place in 1918. But then he was in Durian, so whether he's buried in Durian or buried over here, we still have to find out. So we are looking for that record. We know that his daughter and most of his kids are buried here. And one of the daughters was 110, and she's on the census record and everything. And right near her, there is a lot of grey space that doesn't have a headstone, but nobody's buried there because we know there's already people buried there, and so we kind of think that he might be buried there near his daughter. Yeah. And her name is Bintobell.

CT: What was her name?

C. Binto. Some people call her Binto and I seen it written as Pinto but it's Binto, yeah, Bell.

CT: Did a lot of his children have Islamic names?

C: Yeah. Binto, and um, all the girls did. The girls had some kind of funny names. There were Binto and there were Kato and there was, um, Hester, not the way that we spell it. It was different and later on it became the spelling that the English version of anything that's being spelled. But the names were different.

CT: Ok

C: Yeah. He named them, his kids were not named Mary and Jane, no. There was no Mary and Jane, and his name Bilali passed down and down, and there was many Bilali's. There was his grand-children and his great-grandchildren. The last Bilali died, I think it must be in '72, or something like that, which was one of his great,

great grandson.

CT: The church that we attended today, was it the church that he founded?

C: Not him. His children and grandchildren.

CT: His children and grandchildren.

C: Because he died before that.

CT: Ok. Ok. So he did not form a church?
C: He did not form a church. I don't think he would have formed a church; I will be honest with you. I don't think he would of, because my grandmother would talk about a lot of them having two services, and I would ask her what she meant. They would have a Christian service in the day and have a Muslim service at night.

C: They actually went in the woods and had another service. Deep into the woods, they would have another service. So they had two services, one for the public and one for themselves.

CT: Now Dr. Kly wanted to know where the masons or the shriners was connected in anyway of the church, but he was talking about if Bilali had founded the church ...

C: No he not...

CT:... but was there a lot of masons and shriners connection with.

C: There's Masons. There's a lot of Masons here, there was Messianic order here a long time ago, Messianic's in these areas. That church you went to today is the second location of that church. Now that is where the first African Baptist church originated. It was called First Baptist Church and it was on the West Island place in a little community called Hanging Bull, but they moved it and we also changed the name before that. We changed the name to separate it. Most of the First African Baptist church in this area is the one that have these rituals and so it's called First African Baptist. They took the word and extended it instead of First Baptist because they didn't want it associated with the white churches, the white Baptist churches. They put First African Baptist so that, that way, they could ingrain in the churches there was Christianity, African and

Muslim all rolled into one in the church and it became ours.

CT: Mmhum

C: Yeah and nobody else's. One old Black lady, she died now, she died six years ago, and there was this white lady in church bobbing her head and she said, "honey, let me tell you something. You see the white there, now they go to church with us, they eat with us, they sit with us, but you know the one place that we can still lose them?" I said, "Where?" She said, "In our churches, no matter how they bob their head, when we get in our church services, they cannot catch us, no matter what. We can still lose them every time. " I got to thinking every time I'm sitting in church, (Laughter) and I can't stop thinking about what she said. Now you be watching a white person in church from now on, sitting. (Laughter)

CT: What was Bilali's expectation for the future of the Islamic community? Do you have any idea from your...

C: I have no idea but listening to Grandma growing up, which was one of his granddaughters. Grandma was hard headed, opinionated and liked things her way, and I think her and grandfather, Bilali, was the same way. They didn't conform by too much rules that other people make, and I think grandpa, I mean, if Bilali was still living even today and his children, then this place would have been a different place. Because I don't think, you see, his thing was that he would bow down to no man except God. And so he wouldn't, even as a slave, he didn't bow down to no one, and so they respect him for it and so he couldn't see himself taking a whole lot of their stuff. 'Cause somebody read a book, there is a book called *The Great Oaks* and it is a fictitious romance book and the guy who wrote it, his name was is Ben Ames Williams and he was commissioned to write this book. But you know that all fiction is based on truth, too. And he tell this thing about Bilali in there and about how this white man mistreat Bilali' wife, and that man disappeared and never was found again. My grandmother, she didn't tell anything like that but she told a tale of how one of her ancestors was mistreated by a white man and, um, she slowly kill him by giving him ground glass. Because they didn't take no stuff, and they plot and plan and find some way to get rid of you. One way or the other, they didn't have autopsy back in those days, you know. But I think it would have been a lot different. Yeah.

CT: Does it still exist, some of the Islamic practices that he would have?

C: That he would have. Yeah. Like the church, like praying to the east and so forth like that. Making sure that your feet is washed and a lot of other. You don't think about it in a large lump, and say you can put your hand right on like that, but when you sit down and think about it and go, Oh—we do that. And sometimes we do things and people look at us and say, "Why did you-all do that?" We go, "Oh, we always do that." I have some Islamic brothers who come down and visit me sometime from an order around Athens. They're sitting, and I say something or do something, and they go, "Why did you say that?" And so it just pops up, because it's there, it's a part of us and you can't get rid of it. So we still have more in us than we think that we have. Because to us, it's the norm to do these things and then somebody else from the outside comes in, and points out that it's not the norm.

CT: Well you know what, I see and hear what you are saying and all this is just—I can feel the spirit, right here, now.

C: I sure hope so. The spirit is here. My father and all of the rest of them. My father and my grandfather use to wear, you know, a lot of the Islamic men just wear the amulet and, um, some people call it a amulet instead of however you pronounce it. And they all wore one. I remember that the members would make them wear it around the waistline and I never knew the name 'cause as a child I was raised up, you didn't ask questions. So when grandpapa died, I remember seeing it at momma's house, and I held that thing for the longest… I finally got up enough nerve to open it and I was saying I wonder what's in that little sack and I know momma would—when the little sack, little pouch got dirty—she'd make another one, slide that inside of it and put it back on . I'm going, now, what's in that, and it was a Bible verse that they wore with them at all time and grandpa would say, "with God all things are possible." And that's all there was, just write and put in this little tiny sack and sewed up and wore on their person and all of the men use to wear these. And some families were more into it than other families, although we are all basically cousins, it depends on what side of the family you might of branched from. Some families were more into the old ways and keeping it than others. So it depends on the families. So we kept all that old stuff.

CT: What did you want to say, Halim?

H: What about the use of the hands, the right hands?

C: Oh, (laughter), your right hand, is supposedly ok, but your left hand is cursed, and they said if you are left-handed, you owed the devil a day. At least a day of your life belongs to the devil, if you was left-handed. So we were never forced to use our right hand but we were always told that our left hand—I'm a left-handed person and my mother was a left-handed person, her mother was left-handed. I got a left-handed child, got a couple of left-handed grandchildren. If you were left-handed, you know, you owed the devil one day. It belongs to the devil and we have to pay our dues, someplace down the line. But we were never forced and they didn't put too much emphasis on left hand or right hand when we was growing up, you know. But we had our share of superstition and folklore and everything else, and between all that, all of them had a meeting. You know, just for you to sit down and figure it out. We use to have one teacher use to say, "White man die and leave money, Black man die and leave signs." And I said it would be better if we sat down and decipher those signs.

CT: True, I agree.

C: Because they left them for a reason. And that White man left that money, yes, but that money can be squandered away. Those signs are suppose to last us for a lifetime, and we suppose to pass it on. So they left those signs for a reason, and we tend to ignore them because they have gotten so sophisticated with our computer and flying here and there, that we have forgot the signs. And they left us signs cause that's all they had.

H: Another question that I had is how you feel about honesty, you know, and integrity, and giving your word and all that type of thing?

C: Your word was your bond. My father who died would have talked a little bit at church. The proper thing was, he said, a man—he always said a poor man, and to him and his generation, a black man was a poor man—he said, a poor man got three things going on in life, he said. He got God, his word as a man, and a piece of land. If God saw fit to see to it that you have got a piece of land, he said, brother, keep it, and cherish it, and pass it down. And if you got rid of it for foolishness, he said, your word won't be worth much to fellow man. So the only thing you got left is God, so you better stay on the good side of God for the rest of your life. (Laughter) And so their word was their bond, so they must not be broken, and so that was his belief and he keep up with that. And you get thinking: if you break that bond that you promised somebody, that you shake hand on, your word wasn't worth much, and the whole community around you would always would remember that she promise or he promise, and they break it, and everybody gonna remember, forever. No matter how many good deeds you did, they gonna remember the one that you didn't keep. And having kids out of wedlock was forbidden. Back in those days, even to the time I grew up, and if you did have a child out of wedlock, the church and the elders—you had to marry that young man. Whether there was any love involved, the church would step in, and you were brought before the elders, and you were married, and there were no divorces, either. So that was it. You know, it was a strict thing between the elders and that, and I think that we need some of that back again.

CT: Yeah, we do.

C: We do.

CT: I wanted to sum all of this up. If you could give some kind of word of advice to all of those people in search of their roots, Islamic people, um, how would they go about trying to find that heritage?

C: Well a lot of people that I know, they study the Quran, then you have people that are arguing that one Islamic factor is teaching hate and one Islamic factor is teaching love, and then there is that middle ground group that is trying to balance themselves between both. There is times, as a Black person, you know, that you do feel that you should go back in the old text: a hand for a hand, an eye for an eye. Then you sort of shake your head and go, no, we living in the modern world, we don't do that, somebody punish you. Then you stop and you thinking that common sense set in, you know. I think that people who are Islamic has as much right to practice their beliefs as people who belong to other religions without being intimidated. I mean, this country is suppose to be the country of the free. You suppose to be free to practice your religious beliefs. So I do think people shouldn't berate anybody because they are Jehovah's Witnesses or because they are Islamic or so forth. I went to Sierra Leone and they have a lot of wars over there. I was surprised to see that they had Church and a Mosque all sitting on the same lot and they didn't argue about it. And there are good countries in the world that the Christian sect want to be as far away from the Islamic sect as possible, and I'm going: that's not getting along. What I believe is what I believe, and if I'm not doing you any bodily harm or anything else, then you leave me alone. If I want to pray bending down to God on my knees, and elbow and my head bowed down, then that's my right. And if I want to pray to God by making the sign of the cross and I'm a Catholic, then you leave me alone. And if I want to go to Church because my bell tolls and tells me that it's time to go to Church, then you leave me alone. As long as I basically believe in God, then leave me alone. If I'm treating my fellow man right, and I'm not cheating and killing and cussing and causing confusion—why is it that in this country we have to figure that everybody have to believe in the same thing at the same time in order to get along? That's just ridiculous. God didn't make us all alike. There is a purpose in all of this. We might call it madness today but there is a purpose that he didn't make everybody alike. He didn't make everybody the same color. And I think that if he wanted to do that, he would have did that too, but he didn't. We be separate tones, separate skin tones, separate countries, but we all on the same planet. So we just need to respect people more than we do, and that's basically if you Islamic, respect Christian, and Christian respect Islamic, and we get along all better. In Ireland, they have Catholic Irish and Protestant Irish, but in this country over here we have them both, and I said but how come we never hear anything about them fighting about whether they're Catholic or whether they're Protestant but they're Irish, and somebody go: you know, I haven't thought about that. And so, why do we have to separate everything? Everybody want the same, 'cause they want to, one day, like we say in our Church, "One day go to heaven," to a better place and so, in the meantime, we prepare for it down here. No matter what religion you are, prepare for it down here, so you can have a better place. Some people believe in the afterlife and some people don't.

CT: Right.

C: Black people got a lot—we got enough to deal with, Whether we are Christian or whether we're the right Christian, according to the eyes of other people, and whether we Islamic and whether people will like us if I decide to dress Islamic and portray myself as being of the Islamic faith, and change my name, and whether they will still like me or not. Then inside of all that there is bothering us, there our Africanism pops out. Because we can't get away from that, no matter whether you Islamic or whether you're Catholic or Protestant, it is still there. So that's gonna pop out among everything else. So we got a lot to deal with, and then we have racism and unequalit. We not equal yet in a lot of ways, and so we have all that to deal with. So Black people have a lot of burden to go with. So if I chose my religion and I'm not bothering nobody, like my grandma always say, "just leave the hell me alone." (Laughter) Because I'm not bothering nobody. Respect me as a person, you know, and not saying, no, you shouldn't do this ,or you shouldn't do that. If I'm not running around being a mass murderer and robbing banks and so forth, and a child molester. Like my father say, *what harm, what harm*, like what am I doing, I'm not hurting nobody you know. Yeah, he said, *what harm*, what's the problem, what's wrong. You know and that's it.

CT: Well it's been a wonderful experience and of course I know everybody learnt a lot. (Laughter)

Everybody: Yes!

C: Hey, every time I open my mouth I learn a lot too, so forget it. (Laughter) 'Cause not only that I learn from other people, I learn from myself because while you are talking, you're learning from yourself.

CT: True.

C: You know if you don't learn from yourself while you are talking then you all ready to close your doors also, because while you are talking you are listening to yourself.

CT: Exactly.

C: And while you are listening to yourself, you re going, oh, then you know that actually *do* mean that, or something. So you are actually learning from yourself as well as other people. So it's great, it's not bad at all and, I like....

CT: Well. Yea, um everything's good. Thank you so much

C: Oh, you're welcome.

CT: Thank you, thank you, thank you, I've got to give you a big hug.

CHAPTER FIVE

GULLAH-GEECHEE QUESTION & ANSWER*

ARE ALL PERSONS OF AFRICAN DESCENT IN AMERICA THE SAME?

The one drop rule has tended to overshadow the fact that there is ethnic and cultural diversity within the Black population of the USA. There are African-descent populations in America which have unique cultures and speak a Creole language as their mother tongue. Even within these groups, there are notable dissimilarities. Geechees and other Gullahs living in Georgia, South Carolina and Florida along the southeastern seaboard have cultural dissimilarities as well as cultural similarities to Creoles living in Louisiana along the southern most part of the Mississippi River.[1]

WHO ARE THE GULLAH?

The term Gullah refers to a social group of antebellum people of Black African descent (and their descendants) who experienced chattel slavery in the southeastern part of the USA, as well as their lingua franca.[2]

---

* This article is drawn from a research article by historian J. Vern Cromartie of Contra Costa College, titled "Geechees and Other GUllahs and Maroons: Heroes of the African-American Anti-Slavery Wars", with permission by the author. The Bibliography was compiled by J. Vern Cromartie.
[1] For discussions of the cultural activities of Creole living in Louisiana, see the collection of essays in Hirsch and Logsdon (1992). Two very important essays in that collection include Hall (1992a) and Tregle (1992). See also Hall, (1992b).
[2] For details of the etymology of the term Gullah, see the section below titled "Implications of the terms Gullah and Geechee for Black Culture." Cf. Bascom (1939, 1941); Granger (1940); Savannah Unit (1940); Turner (1941, 1949); Dilliard (1972); Jackson, Slaughter & Black (1974); Wood (1975); Van Sertima (1976); Moore (1980); Baird (1980); Cassidy (1986); Hancock (1986); Jones-Jackson (1986, 1987); Wright (1986); Demerson (1991); Twining and Baird (1991); Demerson (1991); Pollitzer (1999).

WHO ARE THE OUTLYERS?

Although many Africans liberated themselves with the intention of "outlying" on a temporary basis, others intended to stay free on a permanent basis. Liberated Africans who intended to stay out temporarily are referred to as "outlyers"[3] while Africans who joined Maroon communities permanently are called Maroons.

WHERE DID THESE AFRICAN PEOPLES COME FROM?

Many of these enslaved Africans had been kidnapped from their homes along West Africa's Gulf of Guinea.

WHAT LANDS DID THEY INHABIT?

These Africans were dispatched to the area of the eastern seaboard stretching from South Carolina, Georgia and northeastern Florida, up through North Carolina, Virginia, District of Columbia and northeastern Maryland.[4] The central part of the coastal strip that they inhabited consisted mainly of savannah lowlands, which came to be called the "Gullah area".[5] Under the leadership of James Edward

---

[3] The distinction between "Maroon" and "outlyers" draws from Aptheker (1939, 1974) and Franklin and Schweinger (1999). Aptheker (1939) reported that the Norfolk *Herald* of May 12, 1823, used the term outlyers in a news account dealing with "runaway Negroes" (p. 176). Aptheker (1974) also reported that "Strikes were by no means unknown under slavery. The method most commonly pursued was for the Negroes to flee to outlying swamps or forests, and to send back word that only if their demands—perhaps for better food or clothes, or fewer beatings, shorter hours, or even a new overseer—were met (or at least discussed), would they willingly return" (p. 142). In a similar fashion, Fraknlin and Schweinger (1999) related that one of the most common forms of rebelling on the planation was "lying out" (p. 98). In addition, Franklin and Schweinger (1999) related that:
   Slaves who 'layed out' often lived by fishing, hunting, stealing, trading and looting. Sometimes they stayed near relatives or friends, or hid in quarters on neighboring plantations. They encamped near towns and cities, along rivers and streams, or in dense forests and swamps. They stayed alone, in small groups, sometimes in large bands. (p. 100)

[4] Bontemps, (1968); Savanna Unit, (1940); Bancroft, (1931); Douglass, (1962), original work published 1892; Murray-Douglass, (1923). See also Turner (1949); Herskovits (1958); Mannix and Cowley (1965); Wells (1967); Curtin, (1969, 1975); Wood (1974); Wright (1976); Blassingame (1979); Rodney, (1980); Littlefield (1981); Smith, (1985); Bailey, (1992); Miller, (1992).

[5] Turner, (1949); Herskovits, (1958); Blassingame, (1979); Wood, (1975). Wood (1974) has reported that "The influential slave merchant Henry Laurens once wrote to his agent to send 'fine, healthy, young Negro lads & Men, if such [are

Oglethorpe in 1733, European colonists established a permanent settlement in the present-day Savannah, Georgia and Ogeechee River area, which was inhabited by a multivalent clan branch of the Creek Indians.

BY WHAT NAMES WERE THESE AFRICANS KNOWN?

The Africans were known by tribal names such as the Gola (a.k.a. Golla, Galla, Gula and Gulla), Ibo (a.k.a. Igbo, Ebo, Eboe, Aboe and Calabar), Ibibio, Bambara, Mbundu, Mandinka (a.k.a. Mindinga), Mende, Mandingo, Wolof (a.k.a. Jolof) and others, and came to speak a lingua franca called Gullah, which was essentially a mixture of English and African languages, with both French, Spanish and Indian words.

BY WHAT NAMES WERE THEIR INDIAN COMPATRIOTS KNOWN?

Native Americans of Hitchiti-Muskhogean linguistic stock (whose words have a certain phonetic sound and often end in *ee* like Okefenokee, Oconee, Ocmulgee, Ohoopee, Willachoochee, Tallahassee, and Ogeechee). These clans were known variously as the Muskogee, Miccosukee, Yuchi (a.k.a. Uchi, Uche, Uchee, Euchee, Hughchee, and Hog Logee), Tallassee, Tamali, Apalachee, Coweta (a.k.a. Caweta and Kawita), Oconee, Shawnee, Savannah (a.ka. Savanna), Yamascraw, Yamasee (a.k.a. Yamase andYemassee) and Guale as well as Ogeechee (a.k.a. Ogeeche, Ogechee, and Howgechu).[6]

---

available] of any Country except Ebo" (p. 179). Wood (1974) continued: "At another time he stated his desire for slaves from "Gambia & Windward coast [rice regions' . . . or the Angola Men such as are large" (p. 179). In the documentary, "Family Across the Sea," (Carrier, 1991), Joseph Opala emphasizes that Henry Laurens sought enslaved Africans from Sierra Leone. Opala seems to ignore the evidence documented by Wood that Laurens also sought enslaved Africans from Angola and Gambia. The evidence documented by Wood (1974) and Elizabeth Donnan (1900) suggests that many enslaved Africans from Angola and Gambia did indeed end up in South Carolina. However, the evidence gathered by the Savannah Unit (1940) of the Georgia Writers' Project in *Drums and Shadows* indicates that many Ibos did end up enslaved in Georgia. Thus, one should not be surprised to find the place named Ibo Landing on St. Simon's Island, a location where location lore holds that a boatload of Ibos headed for enslavement committed mass suicide or were killed.

[6] Bartram, (1958); Hodge, (1907, 1., 1907b); Gatschat, (1969) original work published 1884; White, (1855); Swanton, (1922); McReynolds, (1957); Nash, (1982); Wright, (1986); Coleman, (1991).

[16]   Bartram, (1958); Sprague, (1858); Hodge, (1907a, 1907b); Moore-Willson, (1910); Porter, (1964); Brandon, (1965); Irvine, (1974); Wright, (1986).

Black Seminoles

**John Jefferson,
John Horse's grandson**

**Seminole woman
with baby, circa 1905**

Mounted Black Seminole Detachment

WHERE DID THE SEMINOLE NATION COME FROM?

William Bartram, writing in the 1700s, has stated the following in his own words:

> And they [Creeks] say, also, that about this period the English were establishing the colony of Carolina, and the Creeks, understanding that they were a powerful, warlike people, sent deputies to Charleston, their capital, offering them their friendship and alliance, which was accepted, and, in consequence thereof, a treaty took place between them, which has remained inviolable to this day: they never ceased war against the numerous and potent bands of Indians, who then surrounded and cramped the English plantations, as the Savannas, Ogeeches, Wapoos, Santees, Yamasees, Utinas, Icosans, Paticas, and others, until they had extirpated them. The Yamasees and their adherents sheltering themselves under the power and protection of the Spaniards of East Florida, they pursued them to the very gates of St. Augustine, and the Spaniards refusing to deliver them up, these faithful intrepid allies had the courage to declare war against them, and incessantly persecuted them, until they entirely broke up and ruined their settlements, driving them before them, till at length they were obliged to retire within the walls of St. Augustine and a few inferior fortified posts on the sea cost.[7]

Around 1750, a Creek Indian chief, who has been called Secoffee as well as "Cowkeeper", led the remnants of what was left of the Ogeechee into the present-day southeast Georgia and northeast Florida area. The Gullah who had liberated themselves from slavery in Georgia combined with this group as well as other contingents of southeastern Indians to form what evolved into the Seminole Nation.[8]

---

[7] Francis Harper, (1958), p. 350. Harper noted that the Ogeechee Indian information contained in her commentary was supplied by J.R.S., which was probably John R. Swanton.

[8] Potter, (1966); Sprague, (1848); Giddings, (1858); Florida Writers' Project, (1939); G atschet, (1884). See also Moore-Willson, (1910); Swanton, (1922); Hodge, (1907b); Pennington, (1930); Porter, (1932, 1943a, 1943b, 1949, 1951, 1952, 1964, 1967); Walker, (1934); Aptheker, (1974); Emerson, (1954); Peithman, (1957); Stoutenburgh, (1960); Crane, (1964); Joseph, (1968); Mahon, (1967); Brinton, (1969); Irvine, (1974); Littlefield, (1977, 1979); Blassingame, (1979); Peters, (1979); Howard, (1984). It should be noted that Porter (2949, 1952, 1967) offers an analysis of the issue concerning whether the historical figures

WHERE DID THE CAPTURED AFRICANS GO TO ESCAPE ENSLAVEMENT?

Many Gullahs in what are the present-day Savannah, Augusta and Brunswick, Georgia areas fled from slavery individually, in pairs and in larger groups. Other Gullahs from the Albany Georgia area and elsewhere later joined them to live as Maroons in locations within, around and below the Okefenokee Swamp—which extends from southeast Georgia to northeast Florida.[9]

Instead of fleeing north, James Madison, William and Ellen Craft, Frederick Douglas and others, many Gullah sought alliances with the Indians to maintain armed struggle against slaveholding Euro-Americans. They carried on guerrilla warfare and encouraged other Blacks to run away from their enslavement and become Maroons. The migration of Gullahs from Georgia to various points south and elsewhere lasted from the 1700s up until the Emancipation Proclamation took effect in the mid-1860s.[10]

HOW DID POPULATION TRANSFER AFFECT THE SEMINOLES?

After determined resistance in the Okefenokee Swamp region by refugee Gullah-speaking Maroons from Georgia plantations and Creek Indians, the war against the colonists began to abate because of their transfer to a new locality. Whereas the Creek Indians, like their kinsmen in Florida, were trying to escape being sent west, the Gullah-speaking Maroons were trying to escape enslavement. In a report to his superior officers, General Thomas S. Jesup repoted in 1839 that:

> ...the Creek Indians have all left the Okefenokee & gone south, there were seven runaway Negroes from Georgia among them, well armed & plenty of ammunition. . . the

---

Secorffee and Cowkeeper were the same individual. He concludes that they were not.

[9] Pennington, (1930); Davis, (1931a, 1931b); Sprague, (1858); "Seminole War", (1837); Hoyt, (1947); Carter, (0000). See also Scarborough, (1933); Flanders (1833); Southall, (1934); Matschat, (1938); Aptheker, (1939, 1974); Porter, (1946); Boyd, (1951); Goggin, (1951); Wax, (1967); Brawley, (1968); Fairbanks, (1973); Littlefield, (1977, 1979); Wood, (1984).

[10] "Extract," (1837); Davis, (1930). Cf. Aptheker, (1939, 1974); Porter, (1945A; 1946B; 1948); Boyd (1951); Proctor, (1965); Bergman and Bergman, (1969); Fairbanks, (1973); Blassingame, (1979); Wood, (1984); Mohr, (1986); Franklin and Moss, (1988); Bennett, (1993); Penningroth, (1997).

Negroes also have left & on their way South burned the
houses in the vicinity.[11]

Instead of fleeing north like John "fed" Brown, James
Madison, William and Ellen Craft, Frederick Douglas and others,
many Gullah sought alliances with the Indians to maintain armed
struggle against slaveholding Euro-Americans. They carried on
guerrilla warfare and encouraged other Blacks to run away from
their enslavement and become Maroons. The migration of Gullahs
from Georgia to various points south and elsewhere lasted from the
1700s up until the Emancipation Proclamation took effect in the
mid-1860s.[12]

Further the Indian allies of the Gullah called all of the Gullahs
"Estelusti".[13] However, to distinguish the Estelusti who fought
alongside them for over one hundred years from the other Gullahs,
their Indian comrades-in-arms probably gave them the war-name
"Geechees" in honor of the Ogeechee clan whose numbers were
decimated by the treachery of the European colonists.[14]

The Gullah-speaking Geechee Maroons, along with their
Indian allies, participated in part of what is called The Seminole
Wars by the Euro-Americans.[15]

[11] Porter, (1943b, p. 410).
[12] "Extract," (1837); Davis, (1930). Cf. Aptheker, (1939, 1974); Porter, (1945A;
1946B; 1948); Boyd (1951); Proctor, (1965); Bergman and Bergman, (1969);
Fairbanks, (1973); Blassingame, (1979); Wood, (1984); Mohr, (1986); Franklin
and Moss, (1988); Bennett, (1993); Penningroth, (1997).
[13] Moore-Willson, (1910); Littlefield, (1977); Wright, (1986).
[14] The Seminole Nation custom of giving war-names is discussed further in the
next two sections of this paper.
[15] Gullah-speakng Geechee Maroons were also engaged in armed struggle
against Euro-American slaveholders before 1817, which some scholars pose
as the official starting date of the First Seminole War. Other scholars list the
official starting date of the First Seminole War with the Federal attack on Fort
Negro. For information on the armed struggle activities of Gullah-speaking
Geechee Maroons at Fort Negro circa 1813-1816 and Fort Mose circa 1738-
1763, see Clinch (1819), Boyd (1951) Cromartie (1987) and Deagan and Landers
(1999). For information on the role of Gullah-speaking Geechee Maroons fighting
against Euro-American slaveholders from Georgia in 1812-1813, see T. Frederick
Davis (1930, 1931a, 1931b). For information on the role of Maroons in the First
Seminole War, see Matschat (1938); Porter, (1951); Brown, (1956); Wright,
(1968). For information on the role of Maroons in the Second Seminole War, see
V.B. Peters, (1979). For information on the role of Maroons in the Third Seminole
War, see Porter (1967); Covington, (1964, 1982). For information on the activities
of Gullah-speaking Maroons after 1842 in such locations as Oklahoma, Texas,
Mexico, Nova Scotia, Bahamas and Liberia,see Goggin, (1946); Littlefield, (1977);
Bullard, (1983); Cromartie, (1987); Opala (1980, 1987?); Mulroy, (1993), Porter,
(1996).

HOW DID THE NATIVES AND GEECHEES COORDINATE THEIR STRUGGLE?

Throughout this long and costly war, Geechees played the decisive roles, not only as warriors but also as strategists, advisors, spies and interpreters as well.[16]

Some Geechees entered the battlefields as chiefs or captains of their own warriors, while others served as lieutenants and warriors under Indian hereditary chiefs and war leaders, and vice versa: some Indians served under Geechee chiefs as well, or nominally under Indian leadership.

TO WHAT EXTENT WAS THIS A WAR BY AFRICANS AGAINST ENSLAVEMENT?

At the outset of the Second Seminole War, the Geechees of the Seminole Confederacy were described as "bold, active and armed". In his history of the Second Seminole War, Captain John T. Sprague wrote the following: "The negroes, from the commencement of the Florida War, have, for their numbers, been the most formidable foe, more blood-thirsty, active and revengeful, than the Indian". Furthermore, whereas General Andrew Jackson had referred to the First Seminole War as "this savage and Negro war", General Thomas S. Jesup referred to the Second Seminole War in the following words, "this . . . is a Negro, not an Indian war".

Although no one, including participants such as Sprague and Jesup, gave the usual military strategic estimation of the number of Gullah (Geechees) they were fighting, sometimes 300, sometimes 1400, the position of this writer is that their numbers were probably significantly higher.[17]

WHAT WERE THE NAMES OF THE GEECHEES WHO FOUGHT ENSLAVEMENT?

Names of male and female Geechee members of the Seminole Confederation (formed between the Indians fleeing the defeated Creek nation and the Gullahs who liberated themselves from enslavement)

---

[16] Giddings, (1858); Cohen, (1836); Marryat, (1839).

[17] Although there is a lot of mystery and confusion in the reports regarding the total population of the Seminole Nation during the three wars, most assert that Black people, which this paper refers to as Gullah-speaking Seminole Maroons, comprised at least one-fifth of that total.

John Horse

included: Abraham (a.k.a. Abram, Abr'm, Yobly, The Prophet, Ibrahim and Souanaffe Tustenukke), Abia, August, Toney Barnett, Polly Barnett, Becky Barnett, Grace Barnett, Lydia Barnett, martinas Barnett, Mary Ann Barnett, Bayal, Betty, Black, Buck, Long Bob, David Bowlegs, Jack Bowlegs, Sam Bowlegs, Ben Bruno, John Caesar, Catherin, Caty, John Cavallo (a.k.a. Gopher John, John Horse, John Coheia and Cowaya), Charles (a.k.a. Tenebo), Cooter, Cornelia, Cosar, Cudjjo, Cuffee, Cuffy, Dambo, Diana, Dinah, Doc, Fay, Andrew Gay (a.k.a. Andrew Gue), Hagar, Hard Times, Harry, Ishmael, Israel, Jenny, Jim, Juba, Juby, Juda, July, Linda, Lucy, Lybby, March, Mary, Matilda, Monday, Mundy, Louis Pacheco (a.k.a. Louis Fatio, Luis Pacheco, and Lewis), Peggy, Pompey, Prince, Queen, Rabbit (a.k.a. Friday), Renty, Sampson, Sandy, Scipio, Smart, Sophy, Sylvia, Tamar, Tamour, Tanneba, Taymour, Teena, Teenar, Tena, Tina, Thursday, Toby, Tunee, Wann (a.k.a. Whan, Juan, Inos, Ino and Inoinophen), William and Washington.[18]

Abraham

WHO IS ABRAHAM [IBRAHIM]?

On June 15, 1837, the *Army and Navy Chronicle* published the following extract of a letter received from a Euro-American officer fighting against the Gullah and Indian Seminole Confederation:

> We have a perfect Talleyrand of the Savage Court in Florida, in the person of a Seminole Negro, called Abraham, who is

---

[18] Mahon, (1967); Littlefield, (1977).

sometimes dignified with the title of "Prophet." He is the Prime Minister and privy councilor of Micanopy; and has, through his master, who is somewhat imbecile, ruled all the councils and actions of the Indians in this region.

Abraham is a non-committal man, with a countenance which none can read, a person erect and active, and in stature over six feet. He was a principal agent in bringing about the peace, having been a commander of the Negroes during the war, and an enemy by no means to be despised. While we lay on the border of Lake To-hop-to-la-ga, and the Big Cypress Swamp, a Negro, Ben, was captured by our horse, and, after detaining him for a day, he was sent out to bring in Abraham, who he said was desirous of peace, and was concealed in the neighborhood.

Abraham made his appearance, bearing a white flag on a small stick which he had cut in the woods, and walked up to the tent of Gen. Jesup with perfect dignity and composure.

He stuck the staff of his flag in the ground, made a salute or bow with his hand, without bending his body, and then waited for the advance of the General, with the most complete self-possession. He has since stated that he was expected to be hung, but concluded to die, if he must, like a man, but that he would make one effort to save his people.[19]

WHAT WERE THE NAMES OF THE NATIVES WHO FOUGHT WITH THE GEECHEES?

Billy Bowlegs

Indian hereditary and war leaders that Geechees fought under during the Second Seminole War included Alligator (a.k.a. Eufalo Mico, Halpatter, Halpatter Tustenugge, and Halpatah Hajo), Euchee Billy (a.k.a. Uchee Billy), Billy Bowlegs (a.k.a. Holata Micco, Halpatter-Micco, Billy Boleck and Bolek), Coacoochee (a.k.a. Wildcat), Cooper (a.k.a. Ossochee, Osuchee, Osuche and Osarchee), Yaha Hajo (a.k.a. Mad Wolf), Hospetarke, Euchee Jack (a.k.a. Uchee

[19] "Seminole War," 1837, p. 378.

Jack), Sam Johnes (a.k.a. Arpeika and Arpiuka), Jumper (a.k.a. Hoethle Ma-tee, Otee, Emathla, Onselmatche), Micanopy (a.k.a. Mikonopi), Octiarche (a.k.a. Ochtiarche and Oktiarche), Osceola (a.k.a. Oseola, Aseola, Asi-Yahola, As-se-se-he-ho-lar and Powell), Otulke-Thloko (a.k.a. Otalke Thlocko and The Prophet), King Philip (a.k.a. Emathla) Tuskinia, and Yaholoochee (a.k.a. Cloud).[20]

Micanopy

WHO LED SOME OF THE COLONIST MILITARY FORCES?

Prominent Euro-American men assigned to state and federal military forces that the Geechees fought against included future president Zachary Taylor and future Civil War hero William Tecumseh Sherman as well as Walker Keither Armistead, Braxton Bragg, Richard Keith Call, Thomas Childs, Duncan L. Clinch, M.M. Cohen, Francis L. Dade, Abraham Eustis, Charles Floyd, Upton S. Frazier (a.k.a. U.S. Frazer and U.S. Fraser), Edmund Pendleton Gaines, Geoorge W. Gardiner, William Selby Harney, Thomas Hilliard, Ethan Allen Hitchcock, James F. Izard, Thomas Sydney Jesup (a.k.a. Thomas Sidney Jesup), William Lindsay, John T. McLaughlin, Jacob Rhett Motte, Edward ord, George Henry preble, Winfield Scott, John T. Sprague, James Sweat, George H. Thomas, David E. Twiggs, and William Jenkins Worth.[21]

HOW WAS THE NAME "GULLAH" ACCOUNTED FOR BY THE EUROPEANS?

According to the *Oxford English Dictionary,* the term Gullah first appeared in the English written literature in the May 12, 1739 issue of the *South Carolina Gazette* in the following manner: "Run away a short well set Negro Man, named Golla Harry" (p. 944). The *Oxford English Dictionary* defines Gullah as follows:

U.S. Also. Golla, Goolah. Conjectured to be either

---

[20] Sprague, (1858); Giddings, (1858); Catlin, (1965); Mahon (1967).
[21] Sprague, (1858); Giddings, (1858); Catlin, (1965; Mahon, (1967).

a shortening of *Angola,* or from a Liberian group of tribes known as Golas. Used *attrib.* Or *absol.* To designate Negroes living on the sea-islands and tide-water coastline of South Carolina and Georgia, and the dialect spoken by them.[22]

HOW DID CONTEMPORARY DEFINITIONS OF GEECHEES ENCOURAGE DISCRIMINATION AGAINST THEM?

The implications of the terms Geechee and Gullah for contemporary African American culture are considerable. Contemporary definitions and etymologies of the terms Geechee and Gullah illustrate distortions and omissions that have led to confusion and mystery. According to the *Oxford English Dictionary,*[23] the term Geechee first appeared in the written English literature in the September 1929 issue of the *National Geographic* in the following manner:

> Among the Negroes living on the Ogeechee River a patois, developed in ante bellum days, has persisted. It impresses the stranger as almost as a new language. The origin of "Geechee," as the patois is called, is explained by the fact that enslaved Africans employed on the old rice plantations were more or less isolated and rarely conversed with their white owners, with the result that their knowledge of English words was slight and the pronunciation of them was bizarre. The "Geechee" negroe speaks in a sort of staccato and always seem excited when talking. His patois is encountered all along the Georgia coast.[24]

Additionally, the Oxford English Dictionary[25] offers the following definition of the term Geechee: "U.S. dial. [f. the name of the Ogeechee river, Georgia.}... Also, a derogatory term for a Negro of the southern United States. Cg. Gullah (p. 417). The *Oxford English Dictionary*'s definition of the term Geechee is both misleading and erroneous. The distinguished historian Peter H. Wood (1974) has

---

[22] *Oxford English Dictionary,* Simpson & Weiner, 1989, p. 944. Porter (1932, 1943a, 1943b, 1944, 1945, 1964); Southall, (1934); Mahon, (1967)
[23] Simpson & Weiner, 1989.
[24] Graves, Ralph, 1926, p. 278
[25] *Ibid.*

made the following statement, "Repeatedly in America, when non-English-speaking groups have imported names which have laudatory or at least neutral implication at first, these gradually have been made common nouns and given a negative connotation by the culturally dominant class" (p. 185). Wood's (1974) statement illustrates the process of that which happened to the term Geechee, that is, the transformation of a positive term into a negative term.

Such statements regarding the term Geechee in the dictionary, which bills itself as the most important of the English language, have important implications.

BIBLIOGRAPHY

A Slave-Trader's Letter Book. (1886, November). *North American Review*, 143, 447-461.

Aptheker, Herbert. (1939). Maroons Within the Present Limits of the United States. *Journal of Negro History*, 24, 167-184.

Aptheker, Herbert. (1974). *American Negro Slave Revolts* (New ed.). New York, NY: International Publishers. (Original work published 1943).

Bailey, Ronald. (1992). The Slave(ry) Trade and the Development of Capitalism in the United States: The Textile Industry in New England. In Joseph E. Inikori and Stanley L. Engerman (Eds.), *The Atlantic Slave Trade: Effects on Economies, Societies, and Peoples in Africa, the Americas, and Europe* (pp. 205-246). Durham, NC: Duke University Press.

Baird, Keith E., & Twining, Mary A. (1980, June). Guy B. Johnson Revisited: Another Look At Gullah. *Journal of Black Studies*, 10, 425-435.

Baird, Keith E., & Twining, Mary A. (1991). Names and Naming in The Sea Islands. In Mary A. Twining & Keith E. Baird (Eds.) *Sea Island Roots* (pp. 37-55). Trenton, NJ: Africa World Press.

Bancroft, Frederic. (1959). *Slave Trading in the Old South*. New York, NY: Frederick Ungar. (Original work published 1831).

Bartram, William. (1958). Travels Through North & South Carolina, Georgia, East & West Florida. In Francis Harper (Ed.), The Travels of William Bartram (Naturalist's Edition) (pp. xxxvii-232). New haven, CT: Yale University Press. (Original work published 1791).

Bascom, William. (1941, January-March). Acculturation Among the Gullah Negroes. *American Anthropologist*, 43, 43-50.

Bascom, William. (1991). Gullah Folk Beliefs Concerning Childbirth. In Mary A. Twining & Keith E. Baird (Eds.), *Sea Island Roots* (pp. 27-36). Trenton, NJ: Africa World Press.

Bennett, Lerone. (1993). *Before the Mayflower* (6th ed). New York, NY: Penguin Books. (Original work published 1962).

Bergman, Peter., & Bergman, Mort N. (1969). *The Chronological History of the Negro in America.* New York, NY: The New American Library, Mentor Books.

Berry, Mary Frances. (1971). Black Resistance/White Law: A History of Constitutional Racism in America. New York, NY: Appleton-Century-Crofts Educational Division, Meredith Corporation.

Blassingame, John. (Ed.). (1977). *Slave Testimony: Two Centuries of Letters, Speeches, Interviews, and Autobiographies.* Baton Rouge, LA: Louisiana State University Press.

Blassingame, John. (1979). *The Slave Community: Plantation Life in the Antebellum South* (Rev. ed.). New York, NY: Oxford University Press.

Bantams, Arena. (1969). Great Slave Narratives. Boston, MA: Beacon Press.

Boyd, mark F. (1951, July). The Seminole war: Its Background and Onset. *Florida Historical Quarterly*, 30, 3-115.

Brandon, William. (196), (Spring). *American Indians and American History. American West, 2.*

Brawley, Benjamin. (1968). *A Social History of the American Negro.* New York, NY: Johnson Reprint Corp. (Original work published 1921).

Brinton, Daniel G. (1969). Notes on the Floridian Peninsula, its Literary History, Indian tribes and Antiquities. New York, NY: Paladin Press. (Original work published 1859).

Brown, Wille James. (1956). *The Negro and Seminole Wars.* Unpublished Master's Thesis, Florida A & M University.

Bullard, Mary. R. (1983). *Black Liberation on Cumberland Island in 1815.* DeLeon Springs, FL: E.O. Painter Printing Co.

Candler, Allen D. (Ed.). *Colonial Records* (Vol. 0). Atlanta, GA:

Carter, Clarence E. (1900). *The Territorial Papers of the United States, the Territory of Florida 1839-1845* (Vol. 26). Washington, DC:

Cassidy, Frederic G. (1986). Some Similarities Between Gullah and Caribbean Creole. In Michael B. Montgomery & Guy Bailey (Eds.), *Language Variety in the South: Perspectives in Black and White* (pp. 30-37). University, AL: University of Alabama Press.

Catlin, George. (1965). *Letters and Notes on the Manners, Customs, and Condition of the North American Indians.* Minneapolis, MN: Ross & Haines. (Original work published 1836).

Clinch, Duncan L. (1819, November 15). Letter to Col. R Butler, dated august 2,

1816. *Daily National Intelligencer*, 7, 2.

Coe, Charles. (1974). *Red Patriots: The Story of the Seminoles*. Gainesville, FL: University of Florida Presses. (Original work published 1898).

Cohen, M.M. (1964). *Notices of Florida and the Campaigns* [Ed. By O.Z. Tyler, Jr.]. Gainesville, FL: University of Florida Press. (Original work published 1836).

Coleman, Kenneth. (Ed.) (1991). *A History of Georgia*. Athens, GA: University of Georgia Press.

Corbitt, D. C. (Ed.). (1937, March). Papers Relating to the Georgia-Florida Frontier, 1784-1800. *Georgia Historical Quarterly*, 21, 75.

Covington, James W. (Ed.). (1964). *The Florida Indians in 1847*. Tequesta, 24, 55

Covington, James W. (1966, July). Episode in the Third Seminole War. *Florida Historical Quarterly*, 45, 45-59.

Covington, James. W. (1982). *The Billy Bowlegs War: 1855-1858 The Final Stand Against the Whites*. Chuluota, FL: The Mickler House Publishers.

Crane, Verner. W. (1964). *The Southern Frontier, 1670-1743*. Ann Arbor, MI: University of Michigan press. (Original work published 1928).

Craven, Frank Wesley. (1971). *White, Red, and Black: The Seventeenth-Century Virginian*. Charlottesville, VA: University Press of Virginia.

Creel, Margaret Washington. (1990). Gullah Attitudes Toward Life and Death. In Joseph E. Holloway (Ed.), *Africanisms in American Culture* (pp. 69-97). Bloomington, IN: Indiana University Press.

Cromartie, J. Vern. (1984). Gullah Strata People: Historical Notes on the Geechees. Unpublished Master's Paper, California State University, Hayward.

Cromartie, J. Vern (nee Jimmie Levern Cromartie). (1987, December). Maroons and Other Forms of Slave Resistance Within the Present Limits of Georgia, 1733-1865: A Chronology. Unpublished Master's Special Project, California State University, Hayward.

Curtin, Phillip D. (1969). *The Atlantic Slave Trade: A Census*. Madison, WI: University of Wisconsin Press.

Curtin, Philip D. (1975). Measuring the Atlantic Slave Trade. In Stanley L. Engerman & Eugene D. Genovese (Eds.), *Race and Slavery in the Western Hemisphere: Quantitative Studies* (pp. 107-128). Princeton, NJ: Princeton University Press.

Davis, T. R. (1900, July). Negro Servitude in the United States. *Journal of Negro History*, 249.

Davis, T. Frederick. (1930, October). United States Troops in Spanish East Florida,

1812-1813 Part II. *Florida Historical Quarterly*, 9, 96-116.

Davis, T. Frederick. (1931a, January). United States Troops in Spanish East Florida, 1812-1813 Part III. *Florida Historical Quarterly*, 9, 135-155.

Davis T. Frederick. (1931b, April). United States Troops in Spanish East Florida, 1812-1813 Part IV. *Florida Historical Quarterly*, 9, 259, 278.

Davis, George A.. Donaldson, O. Fred. (1975). *Blacks in the United States: A Geographic Perspective*. Boston, MA: Houghton Mifflin Co.

Deagan, Kathleen, & Landers, Jane. (1999). Fort Mose: Earliest free African-American Town in the United States. In Theresa A. Singleton (Ed.), *"I, Too, Am America": Archaeological Studies of African-American Life* (pp. 261-282). Charlottesville, VA: University Press of Virginia.

Demerson, Bamidele Agbasegbe. (1991). Family Life on Wamalaw Island. Sea island Roots. In Mary A. Twining & Keith E. Baird (Eds.) *Sea Island Roots* (pp. 57-87). Trenton, NJ: Africa World Press.

Dilliard, J.L. (1972). *Black English*. New York, NY: Random House.

Donnan, Elizabeth. (Ed.). (1935). *Documents Illustrative of the History of the Slave Trade to America* (Vol. 4). Washington, DC: Carnegie Institution of Washington.

Douglass, Frederick. (1962). *Life and Times of Frederick Douglass* (Revised Edition). New York, NY: Collier Books. (Original work published 1892).

Du Bois, W. E. B. (1892). The Enforcement of the Slave-Trade Laws. In *Annual Report of the American Historical Association for the Year 1891* (Senate M isc. Dec. 173, 52nd Cong., 1st Sess., 1982) (pp. 163-174). Washington, Dc: Government Printing Office.

Du Bois, W. E. B. (1969). *The Suppression of the Atlantic Slave Trade to the United States, 1638-1870*. New York, NY: Schocken Books. (Original work published 1896).

Du Bois, W. E. B. (1903). *The Souls of Black Folk: Essays and Sketches*. Chicago, Il: McClurg.

Emerson, William C. (1954). *The Seminoles: Dwellers of the Everglades*. New York, NY: Exposition Press.

Extract of a letter received by a gentleman in Savannah... (1837, June 15). *Army and Navy Chronicle*, 4, 379.

Fairbanks, Charles H. (1973). *The Florida Seminole People*. Phoenix, AZ: Indian Tribal Series.

Fairbanks, Charles H. (1974). *Ethnohistorical Report on the Florida Indians*. New York, NY: Oxford University Press.

Federal Writers' project. (Ed.). (1939). *Florida: A Guide to the southernmost State.* New York, NY: Oxford University Press.

Flanders, Ralph Betts. (1933). *Plantation Slavery in Georgia.* Chapel Hill, NC: University of North Carolina Press.

Floyd, John. (1949). Letters of John Floyd, 1813-1838. *Georgia Historical Quarterly,* 33, 228-269.

Foner, Philip S. (1975). *History of Black Americans: From Africa to the Emergence of the Cotton Kingdom.* Westport, CT: Greenwood Press.

Foreman, Carolyn T. (1955-1956, Winter). Billy Bowlegs. *Chronicles of Oklahoma, 33.*

Foster, Laurence. (1978). *Negro-Indian Relationships in the Southeast.* New York, NY: AMS (Original Work published 1935).

Franklin, John Hope, & Schweninger. (1999). *Runaway Slaves: Rebels on the Plantation.* New York, NY: Oxford University Press.

Gatschet, Albert S. (1884). *A Migration Legend of the Creek Indians, with a Linguistic, Historic, and Ethnographic Introduction.* Philadelphia, PA: D. G. Brinton.

Gatschet, Albert S. (1888). Tchikilli's Kashita Legend in the Creek and Hitchiti Languages with a critical Commentary and Full Glossaries to Both Texts. *Transactions of the Academy of Science of St. Louis,* 5, 33-239.

Giddings, Joshua R. (1858). *The Exiles of Florida: Or, The Crimes Committed Against the Maroons Who Fled from South Carolina and Other Slave States Seeking Protection Under Spanish Laws.* Columbus, OH: Follett, Foster and Co.

Goggin, John M. (1946). The Seminole Negroes of Andros Island, Bahamas. *Florida Historical Quarterly,* 24, 201-206.

Granger, Mary. (1972). Introduction. In Savannah Unit, Georgia Writers Project, Work Projects Administration. (pp. xxi-xxiv). *Drums and Shadows: Survival Studies Among the Georgia Coastal Negroes.* Athens, GA: University of Georgia Press. (Original work published 1940).

Graves, Ralph A. (1926, September). Marching Through Georgia Sixty Years After. *National Geographic Magazine,* 50, 259-311.

Guthrie, Patricia. (1977). Catching Sense: The Meaning of Plantation Membership on St. Helena Island, South Carolina. Ph.D. dissertation, University of Rochester. [Holloway, 1990, p. 95]

Guthrie, Patricia. (1980, February 21). Praise House Worship and Litigation Among Afro-Americans on a South Carolina Sea Island., paper presented at the sixth Annual Martin Luther King Lecture Series, Purdue University. [Holloway, 1990, p. 95]

Hall, Gwendolyn Midlo. (1992a). The Formation of Afro-Creole Culture. In Arnold

R. Hirsch and Joseph Logsdon (Eds.), *Creole New Orleans: Race and Americanization* (pp. 58-87). Baton Rouge, LA: Louisiana State University Press.

Hancock, Ian. (1986). On the Classification of Afro-Seminole. In Michael B. Montgomery & Guy Bailey (Eds.), *Language variety in the South: perspectives in Black and White* (pp. 85-101). University, AL: University of Alabama Press.

Harding, Vincent. (1981). *There is a River: The Struggle for Black Freedom in America*. New York, NY: Harcourt Brace Jovanovich.

Harper, Francis. (1958). *Preface. In William Bartram, the Travels of William Bartram* (Naturalist's Edition Edited by Francis Harper). New Haven, CT: Yale University Press.

Hawkins, Benjamin. (1848). *A Sketch of the Creek Country in the Years 1798 and 1799* [Collections of the Georgia Historical Society, Vol. 3, Pt. 1]. Savannah, GA: The Society.

Herskovits, Melville J. (1958). *The Myth of the Negro Past*. Boston, MA: Beacon Press. (Original work published 1941).

Hodge, Frederick W. (1907a). *Handbook of American Indians of North Mexico* (Vol. 1). New York, NY: Government Printing Office.

Hodge, Frederick W. (1907b). *Handbook of American Indians North of Mexico* (Vol. 2). New York, NY: Government Printing Office.

Holloway, Joseph E. (Ed.). (1990). *Africanisms in American Culture*. Bloomington, IN: Indiana University Press.

Holloway Joseph E., and Vass, Winifred K. (1993). *African American English*. Bloomington, IN: Indiana University Press.

Howard, James H. (1984). *Oklahoma Seminoles Medicines, Magic, and Religion*. Norman, OK: University of Oklahoma Press.

Hoyt, Edwin P. (1973). *African Slavery*. New York, NY: Abelard-Schuman.

Irvine, Keith. (Ed.). (1974). *Encyclopedia of Indians of the Americas* (Vol. 1). St Clair Shores, MI: Scholarly Press.

Jackson, Juanita; Slaughter, Sabra; & Herman Blake. (1974, March). The Sea Islands as a Cultural Resource, *Black Scholar*, 5, 32-39.

Johnston, James Hugo. (1929, January). Documentary Evidence of the Relations of Negroes and Indians. *Journal of Negro History*, 14, 37-40.

Jones-Jackson, Patricia A. (aka Patricia Ann Jones Jackson). (1978). The Status of Gullah: an Investigation of Convergent Processes. Ph.D. dissertation, University of Michigan [Pollitzer, 1999, p. 277]

Jones-Jackson, Patricia A. (1977, September). Alive: African Tradition on the

Sea islands. *Negro Historical Bulletin*, 46, 95-96, 106. [Twining and Baird, 1991, p. 173]

Jones-Jackson, Patricia A. (1983, March). Contemporary Gullah Speech. *Black Scholar*, 13, 3. [Twining & Baird, 1991, p 173]

Jones-Jackson, Patricia A. (1986). On the Status of Gullah on the Sea Islands. In Michael B. Montgomery & Guy Bailey (Eds.), *Language Variety in the South: Perspectives in Black and White* (pp. 63-72). University, AL: University of Alabama Press.

Jones-Jackson, Patricia A. (1987). *When Roots Die: Endangered Traditions on the Sea Islands*. Athens, GA: University of Georgia Press.

Josephy, Alvin M., Jr. (1968). *The Indian Heritage of America*. New York, NY: Alfred Knopf.

Joyner, Charles W. (1977). Slave Folklife on the Waccamaw Neck: Antebellum Black Culture in the South Carolina Lowcountry. Ph.D. Dissertation, University of Pennsylvania. [Pollitzer, 1999, p. 278]

Katz, William Loren. (1986). *Black Indians: A Hidden Heritage*. New York, NY: Atheneum.

Kly, Yussuf N. (1998). The Gullah War: 1739-1858. In Marquetta L. Goodwine and The Clarity Press Gullah Project. (Eds.), *The Legacy of Ibo Landing: Gullah Roots of African American Culture* (pp. 19-53). Atlanta, GA: Clarity press, Inc.

Kly, Yussuf N. (1999, May/June). The Gullah wars: The Hidden American Anti-Slavery War... *Islamic Horizons*, 28, 42, 45.

Koger, Larry. (1985). *Black Slave Owners, 1790-1860*. Jefferson, NC: McFarland and Co.

Krogman, Wilton Marion. (1934, October). *The Racial Composition of the Seminole Indians of Florida and Oklahoma*. Journal of Negro History, 19, 421-422.

Irvine, Keith. (Ed.). (1974) *Encyclopedia of Indians of the Americas* (Vol. 1). St Clair Shores, MI: Scholarly Press Inc.

Laurens, Henry. (1965-1985). *Papers of Henry Laurens* [Eds. Phillip M. Hamer, George C. Rogers, and David R. Chestnut]. [Volumes 1-13]. Columbia, SC: Published for the South Carolina Historical Society by the University of South Carolina Press.

Littlefield, Daniel F. (1979). *Africans and Creeks: from the Colonial Period to the Civil War*. Westport, CT: Greenwood Press.

Loring, E.N. (1976). Charles C. Jones Missionary to Plantation Slaves, 1835-1847. Ph.D. dissertation, Vanderbilt University. [Twining & Baird, 1999, p. 173]

Mahon, John K. (1967). *History of the second Seminole War, 1835-1842*. Gainesville, FL: University of Florida Press.

Mannix, Daniel P., & Cowley, Malcolm. (1962). *Black Cargoes: A History of the Atlantic Slave trade, 1518-1865.* New York, NY: The Viking Press.

Marbury, Horatio, & Crawford, William H. (Eds.). (1802). *Digest of the Laws of Georgia.* Savannah, GA: Seymour, Woolhopter, & Stebbins.
Marryat, Frederick. (1839). *A Diary in America* (Vol. 3, Part 2). London, England. [pp. 238, 250] cf. wood (1974), p. 115.

Matschat, Cecile Hulse. (1938). *Suwannee River: Strange Green Land.* New York, NY: The Literary Guild of America, Inc.

McReynolds, Edwin C. (1957). *The Seminoles.* Norman, Ok: University of Oklahoma Press.

Miller, Joseph C. (1992). The Numbers, Origins, and Destinations of Slaves in the Eighteenth-Century Angolan Slave Trade. In Joseph E. Inikori and Stanley L. Engerman (Eds.), *The Atlantic Slave Trade: Effects on Economies, Societies, and Peoples in Africa, the Americas, and Europe* (pp. 77-115). Durham, NC: Duke University Press.

Milligan, John D. (1974, Spring). Slave Rebelliousness and the Florida Maroon. *Prologue,* 6.

Mohr, Clarence L. (1986). *On the Threshold of Freedom: Masters and Slaves in Civil War Georgia.* Athens, GA: University of Georgia Press.

Montgomery, C. J. (1908, October-December). Survivors From the Cargo of the Slave Yacht Wanderer. *American Anthropologist,* 10, 611-623.

Moore, Janie Gilliard. (1980), June. A James island Childhood: Africanisms Among Families of the Sea Islands of Charleston, South Carolina. *Journal of Black Studies,* 10, 467-480.

Moore-Willson, Minnie. (1910). The Seminoles of Florida. New York, NY: Moffat, Yard and Co.

Morse, Jedidiah. (1822). A Report to the Secretary of War of the United States on Indian Affairs.

Motte, Jacob R. (1953). *Journey into the Wilderness: An Army Surgeon's Account of Life in Camp and Field during the Creek and Seminole Wars, 1836-1838* [Ed. By James F. Sunderman]. Gainesville, GA: University of Florida Press.

Mulroy, Kevin. (1993). *Freedom on the Border: The Seminole Maroons in Florida, the Indian Territory, Coahuila and Texas.* Lubbock, TX: Texas Tech University Press.

Murray-Douglass, Anna. (1923, January). My mother as I recall Her. *Journal of Negro History,* 8.

Nash, Gary B. (1982). *Red, White, and Black: The Peoples of early America* (2 ed). Englewood Cliffs, NJ: Prentice-Hall.

Neill, Wilfred T. (1956). *The Story of Florida's Seminole Indians* (2 ed.). St. Petersburg, FL: Great Outdoors Publishing Co.

Oglethorpe, James. (1873). Letters from General Oglethorpe to the Trustees of the colony and Others, from October, 1735 to August, 1744. *Georgia Historical Collections.* (Vol. 3). Savannah, GA: Georgia Historical Society.

Opala, Joseph A. (1980). *A Brief History of the Seminole Freedmen.* Austin, TX: University of Texas African and Afro-American Studies and Research Center, Series 2, No. 3.

Opala, Joseph A. (1981). Seminole-African relations on the Florida Frontier. *Papers in Anthropology* [University of Oklahoma], 22, 11-52.

Opala, Joseph A. (1987?). *The Gullah: Rice, Slavery, and the Sierra Leone-American Connection.* Freetown, Sierra Leone: USIS.

Peithman, Irvin M. (1957). *The Unconquered Seminole Indians.* St. Petersburg, FL: Great Outdoors Publishing Co.

Pennington, Edgar Legare. (1930). East Florida in the American Revolution, 1775-1778. *Florida Historical Quarterly*, 9, 24-46.

Penningroth, Dylan. (1997, September). Slavery, Freedom, and Social Claims in Liberty County, Georgia, 1850-1880. *Journal of American History*, 84, 405-435.

Perdue, Theda. (1993). *Nations Remembered: An Oral History of the Cherokees, Chickasaws, Choctaws, Creeks, and Seminoles in Oklahoma, 1865-1907.* Norman, OK: University of Oklahoma Press.

Peters, Richard, (Ed.). (1845) *The Public Statues at Large of the United States of America.* Boston, MA: Charles C. Little and James Brown.

Peters, Virginia Bergman. (1979). *The Florida Wars.* Hamden, CT: Archon Books.

Pinckney, Elise. (Ed.). (1972). *The Letterbook of Eliza Lucas Pinckney 1739-1762.* Chapel Hill, NC: University of North Carolina Press.

Ploksi, Harry A., Williams, James. (1983). *The Black American Reference Book.*

Pollitzer, William S. (1993). The relationship of the Gullah-Speaking People of Coastal South Carolina and Georgia to Their African Ancestors, *Historical Methods*, 25, 53-67.

Pollitzer, William S. (1999). *The Gullah People and Their African Language.* Athens, GA: University of Georgia Press.

Porter, Kenneth W. (1932, July). Relations Between Negroes and Indians Within the Present Limits of the United States, *Journal of Negro History*, 17, 287-367.

Porter, Kenneth W. (1941). Abraham. *Phylon*, 2, 107-116.

Porter, Kenneth W. (1943a, January). Three Fighters for Freedom. *Journal of Negro History*, 28, 51-72.

Porter, Kenneth W. (1943b, October). Florida Slaves and Free Negroes in the Seminole War, 1835-1842. *Journal of Negro History*, 28, 390-421.

Porter, Kenneth W. (1944). Seminole Flight from Fort Marion. *Florida Historical Quarterly*, 22, 112-133. or 113-133.

Porter, Kenneth W. (1945a, January). *Negroes and the East Florida Annexation Plot. Journal of Negro History*, 30, 9-29.

Porter, Kenneth W. (1945b). Notes on Seminole Negroes in the Bahamas. *Florida Historical Quarterly*, 24.

Porter, Kenneth W. (1946a, April). John Caesar: Seminole Negro Partisan. *Journal of Negro History*, 31, 190-207.

Porter, Kenneth W. (1946b, July). The Negro Abraham. *Florida Historical Quarterly*, 25.

Porter, Kenneth W. (1947, July). The Episode of Osceola's Wife: Fact or Fiction? *Florida Historical Quarterly*, 26.

Porter, Kenneth W. (1948, January). Negroes on the Southern Frontier, 1670-1763. *Journal of Negro History*, 33, 53-78.

Porter, Kenneth W. (1949, April). The founder of the 'Seminole Nation' Secoffee or Cowkeeper. *Florida Historical Quarterly*, 27, 362-384.

Porter, Kenneth W. (1950, April). Negro Guides and Interpreters in the early Stages of the Seminole War, December 28, 1835-March 6, 1837. *Journal of Negro History*, 35, 174-182.

Porter, Kenneth W. (1951, July). Negroes and the Seminole War, 1817-1818. *Journal of Negro History*, 36, 249-280.

Porter, Kenneth W. (1952, April). The Cowkeeper Dynasty of the Seminole Nation. *Florida Historical Quarterly*, 30, 341-349.

Porter, Kenneth W. (196), November). Negroes and the Seminole War, 1835-1842. *Journal of Southern History*, 30, 427-450.

Porter, Kenneth W. (1967, January). Billy Bowlegs (Holata Micco) in the Seminole Wars. *Florida Historical Quarterly*, 45, 219-242, 391-401.

Porter, Kenneth W. (1996). *The Black Seminoles: History of a freedom-Seeking People* (revised and ed. By Alcione M. Amos & Thomas P. Senter). Gainesville, FL: University Press of Florida.

Potter, Woodburne. (1966). *The War in Florida*. Ann Arbor, MI: University

Microfilms. (Original work published 1836).

Price, Richard (Ed.). (1979). *Maroon Societies: Rebel Slave Communities in the Americas* (2ⁿᵈ ed.). Baltimore, MD: John Hopkins University Press.

Proctor, William G., Jr. (1956), March). Slavery in Southwest Georgia. *Georgia Historical Quarterly*, 49, 1-22.

Rodney, Walter. (1980). *A History of the Upper Guinea Coast 1545 to 1800.* New York, NY: Monthly Review Press.(Original work published 1970).

Savannah Unit, Georgia Writers' Project, Work Projects Administration. (1972). *Drums and Shadows: Survival Studies Among the Georgia Coastal Negroes.* Athens, GA: University of Georgia Press. (Original work published 1940).

Scarborough, Ruth. (1933). *The Opposition to Slavery in Georgia prior to 1861.* Nashville, TN:

Sell, Edward S. (1961). *Geography of Georgia.* Chattanooga, TN: Harlow Publishing Corp.

Seminole War. (1837, June 15). *Army and Navy Chronicle*, 378.

Sills, David. (Ed.). (1991). *International Encyclopedia of the Social Sciences.* New York, NY: Macmillan.

Simpson, John A. & Weiner, Edmund S. C. (Eds.). (1989). *The Oxford English Dictionary.* New York, NY: Oxford University Press.

Smith, Julia Floyd. (1985). *Slavery and Rice Culture in Low Country Georgia, 1750-1860.* Knoxville, TN: University of Tennessee Press.

Southall, Eugene p. (1934, January). Negroes in Florida Prior to the Civil war. *Journal of Negro History*, 19, 81.

Sprague, John T. (1848). *The Origin, progress, and Conclusion of the Florida War.* New York, NY: D. Appleton & Co.

Stephens, William. (1906). A Journal of the Proceedings in Georgia Beginning October 20, 1737. *Colonial Records of the State of Georgia* (Vol. 4). Atlanta, GA.

Stoutenburgh, John L. (1960). *Dictionary of the American Indian.* New York, NY: Philosophical Library.

Sturtevant, William C. (1953). *Chakaika and the "Spanish Indians".* Tequesta, 13, 35-74.

Sturtevant, William C. (1955, January-April). Notes on Modern Seminole Traditions of Osceola. *Florida Historical Quarterly*, 33, 206-216.

Swanton, John R. (1922). *Early History of the Creeks and Their neighbors* [Bureau of American Ethnology Bulletin No. 73]. Washington, DC: Government

Printing Office.

Swanton, John R. (1924-25a). Social Organization and Social usages of the Indians of the Creek Confederacy.

Swanton, John R. (1924-25b). Religious Beliefs and Medical Practices of the Creek Indians.

Swanton, John R. (1946). *The Indians of the Southeastern United States* [Bureau of American Ethnology Bulletin 137]. Washington, DC: Government Printing Office.

Tanner, Earl C. (Ed.). (1952, January). The Early Career of Edwin T. Jenckes: A Florida Pioneer of the 1830s. *Florida Historical Quarterly*, 30, 260-275.

Thorpe, Earl. (1971). *Black Historians: A Critique*. New York, NY: William Morrow and Company, Inc.

Tucker, Phillip Thomas. (1992, Spring). John Horse: Forgotten African-American Leader of the second Seminole War. *Journal of Negro History*, 77, 74-83.

Turner, Lorenzo Dow. (1941, September). Linguistics Research and African Survivals. In Melville J. Herskovits (Ed.), *The Interdisciplinary Aspects of Negro Studies* [American Council of Learned Societies Bulletin No. 32] (pp. 68 890. Washington, DC: American Council of Learned Societies.

Turner, Lorenzo Dow. (1949). *Africanisms in the Gullah Dialect*. Chicago, IL: University of Chicago Press.

Twining, Mary Arnold. (1975). Sources in the Folklore and Folklife of the Sea Islands. *Southern Folklore Quarterly*, 39, 135-150. [Holloway, 1990, p. 92]

Twining, Mary Arnold. (1977). An Examination of African Retentions in the Folk Culture of the South Carolina and Georgia Sea Islands. Ph.D. dissertation, Indiana University. [Pollitzer, 1999, p. 289]

Twining, Mary Arnold, & Baird, Keith E. (1991). Sea Island Culture: Matrix pf the African American Family. In Mary A. Twining & Keith E. Baird (Eds.). *Sea Island Roots* (pp. 1-18). Trenton, NJ: Africa World Press.

UNESCO. (1969). *Four Statements on the Race Question*. Paris, France: Author.

Van Sertima, Ivan. (1976). My Gullah Brother and I: Exploration into Community's Language and Myth through Its oral Tradition. In Deborah Sears Harrison and Tom Trabasso (Eds.), *Black English: A Seminar* (pp. 123-146). Hillsdale, NJ: Lawrence Erlbaum Associates, Publishers.

Vanstory, Burnette. (1956). *Georgia's Land of the Golden Isles*. Athens, GA: University of Georgia Press.

Vass, Winifred Kellersberger. (1979). *The Bantu Speaking Heritage of the United States*. Los Angeles, CA: Centre for Afro-American Studies, UCLA. [Holloway & Vass, 1993, p. 186]

Walker, Laura S. (1934). *History of Ware County, Georgia.* Macon, GA: J. W. Burke Co. Publishers.

Wax, Darold D. (1967, March). Georgia and the Negro Before the American Revolution. *Georgia Historical Quarterly, 51.*

Wells, Thomas Henderson. (1967). *The Slave Ship Wanderer.* Athens, GA: University of Georgia Press.

Wesley, Charles H. (1942, April). Manifests of Slave Shipments along the Waterways, 1808-1864. *Journal of Negro History, 27.*

White, George. (1855). *Historical Collections of Georgia.* New York, NY: Pudney & Russell, Publishers.

Wilcox, C. de Witt. (1909). Letters of Don Manuel de Montiano, Siege of St Augustine. *Georgia Historical Collections* (Vol. 7, Pt. 1). Savannah, GA: Georgia Historical Society.

Willis, William S. Jr. (1963, July). Divide and Rule: Red, White and Black in the Southeast. *Journal of Negro History*, 48, 157-176.

Wood, Peter. (1974). *Black Majority: Negroes in Colonial South Carolina from 1670 through the Stono Rebellion.* New York, NY: W.W. Norton & Company, Inc.

Wood, Betty. (1984). *Slavery in Colonial Georgia*, 1730-1775. Athens, GA: University of Georgia Press.

Work, Monroe N. (1905, November). Some Geechee Folklore. *Southern Workman*, 34, 633-635.

Work, Monroe N. (1905, December). Some Geechee Folklore. *Southern Workman*, 34, 696-697.

Wright, J. Leitch, Jr. (1968). A Note on the First Seminole War as Seen by the Indians, Negroes, and Their British Advisors. *Journal of Southern History*, 34, 565-575.

Wright, J. Leitch, Jr. (1971). Lord Dunmore's Loyalist Asylum in the Floridas. *Florida Historical Quarterly*, 49, 370-379.

Wright, J. Leitch, Jr. (1976, April). Blacks in British East Florida. *Florida Historical Quarterly*, 54.

Wright, J. Leitch, Jr. (1986). *Creeks and Seminoles: Destruction and Regeneration of the Muscogulge People.* Lincoln, NB: University of Nebraska Press.

CHAPTER SIX

CAPTURED AFRICAN PRISONERS OF WAR

A SALUTE TO THE KNOWN AND UNKNOWN
AMONG THE VAST MAJORITY
WHO SOUGHT FREEDOM
AND HUMAN DIGNITY

MAY GOD BE PLEASED WITH THEM

Troops Commanded by Major General Thomas S. Jesup, in 1836 and 1837
From 25 Cong., 3 Sess., *Executive Document 225*, pp. 66-69.

List A

Name	Sex	Est. Age	Remarks
Jacob	Male	25 years	Wounded in right knee
Rina	Female	18 years	Wife to Jacob
Venice	Female	2 years	Child of Jacob
Claudia	Female	2 months	Child of Jacob, died May 27, 1837
Jane	Female	40 years	Mother to Rina and Molly
Molly	Female	23 years	Mother to Billy
Billy	Male	12 years	
Chloe	Female	19 years	Sister to Jacob, mother to Suah and Dennis
Suah	Female	2 years	
Dennis	Male	1 year	

Source: Library of Congress

Pompey	Male	70 years
Dolly	Female	50 years Wife to Pompey
Lilla	Female	20 years Mother to Tom and
Bella		
Tom	Male	11 years
Bella	Female	9 years
Hagar	Female	30 years
Ned	Male	3 years
Fanny	Female	27 years Mother to Charles and
		Margaret
Charles	Male	6 years
Margaret	Female	4 years
Sylvia	Female	-
Buno	Male	19 years
Peggy	Female	45 years Daughter to Pompey
		and Dolly, mother to Hagar
Bob	Male	30 years
Margaret	Female	21 years
Cyrus	Male	13 years
Rose	Female	70 years Grandmother to
		Jacob and Chloe; sold to Mr.
		Forrester, of Six-mile Creek,
		to Bowlegs, several years since
Juba	Female	20 years Cousin to Jacob
Ned	Male	19 years
Noble	Male	23 years
Phebe	Female	33 years Jacob's uncle's wife,
		mother to Toney and Argus
Toney	Male	11 years
Argus	Male	7 years
Nelly	Female	20 years Mother to Scipio
Scipio	Female	3 years
Sandy	Male	1 year
Elsey	Female	25 years Mother to Katy
Katy	Female	3 years
Dick	Male	55 years Said to be the
		property of Colonel Humphreys
Tena	Female	50 years Mother to Susan and
		Nancy, raised with Indians
Susan	Female	14 years
Nancy	Female	9 years
Linda	Female	8 years
Mary	Female	24 years Daughter to Tena,
		mother to Pussy, Ishmael,
		Cyrus, Tamar, and Scipio
Pussy	Female	10 years
Ishmael	Male	6 years
Cyrus	Male	5 years

Tamar	Female	3 years
Scipio	Male	1 year
Patty	Female	33 years Daughter to Tena, mother to Lucy, Pompey and Matilda
Lucy	Female	7 years
Pompey	Male	4 years
Matilda	Female	3 years
Katy	Female	25 years
Eliza	Female	20 years
Ben	Male	40 years Father to Flora, Patty, Charles, Polly, Joe, Betty, Elsey, Robert; one of the most important and fluential characters among the Indian Negroes, never had a white master
Jane	Female	35 years Wife to Ben
Flora	Female	13 years
Patty	Female	12 years
Charles	Male	11 years
Polly	Female	9 years
Joe	Male	7 years
Betty	Female	4 years
Elsey	Female	3 years
Robert	Male	½ month
Betsey	Female	45 years
Washington	Male	11 years
Rachel	Female	25 years
Hetty	Female	
Fanny	Female	
Joseph	Male	
Ino [1]	Male	45 years Father to Toby and Catherine; commander of the Negro force on the Withlacoochee; the chief counselor among the Negroes, and the most important characters
Eliza	Female	35 years Wife to Ino
Toby	Male	20 years
Catherine	Female	12 years
Nancy	Female	1 year, Rachel's child
Katy	Female	25 years Defect in right eye; cousin to Murray, mother to Fanny; said to be property of Colonel Humphreys
Fanny	Female	2 years
Susan	Female	30 years

Ben	Male	22 years
Jacob	Male	24 years
Mundy	Male	20 years
Murray	Male	35 years Owned by Colonel Crowell, and claimed by Nelly Factor, the best guide in the nation
Prince	Male	24 years
Tony	Male	25 years Hostile, qualified to lead in an insurrection
Toby	Male	32 years Hostile, qualified to lead in an insurrection
Peter	Male	15 years
Pompey	Male	60 years
Jacob, 2nd	Male	20 years
Daley	Male	22 years
Mundy	Male	1 ½ years Died May 11, 1837
George	Male	1 year Died May 23, 1837
Philip	Male	4 years Died May 17, 1837
Morris	Male	1 year Died May 31, 1837
Lydia	Female	60 years Died May 11, 1837
Abraham	Male	50 years The principal Negro chief; supposed to be friendly to the whites
Toney Barnett	Male	36 years Said to be a good soldier, and an intrepid leader. He is the most cunning and intelligent Negro we have here. He is married to the widow of the former chief of the nation.
Polly Barnett	Male	36 years
Beckey	Female	2 years
Grace	Female	6 years
Lydia	Female	5 years
Mary Ann	Female	3 years
Martinas	Male	1 year

Negroes Brought in by August and Latty at Fort Jupiter to General Jesup who Offered Freedom to all who should Separate From Seminoles and Surrender

From National Archives Record Group 94, Records of the Office of the Adjutant General, *General Jesup's Papers*, Box 15

List B

Name   Remarks

Name	Status	Name	Status
July	Killed in Florida	Sarah	
		Dick	
Tina		Ismael	
Susan		Peggy	
Nanny		Tamer	
Nelly		March	
Sampson		Kokee	
Kistooa		Hager	
Jenny		Pussey	
Norata		Dosha	
Pond		Harriet	
Rosenta		Tennibo	
Kuntusee		Long Bob	Dead
Phillis		Old John	
Robert		Flora	
Joe		William	
Sandy	Dead	Jim	
Lucy		Rose	
Dembo		Milly	
Thomas		Cesar	
Elsy		Eve	
Rose		Phillis	
Mique		Jeffrey	
Hannah		Milly	
Frank		Nanny	
July Jr.		Betsy	
Liddy		Joe	
Sandy		Titus	
Hetty		William	
Rofina		Cudjo	
Linda		Ben	
Nancy		Rudy	
Rose		Jim	
Sarah		Charlotte	
Traphom		Harriet	
Lewis		Hannah	
Nancy		Nancy	
Bacchus		Sancho	
Susan		Fanny	
Thomas		Prince	
Jessee		Ned	
Monday		Ned 2nd	
Tom		Jack	
Old Primus		Rose	
Flora		Plenty	Dead
Queen		Sally	
Abia		Rachael	

Jack	Sold to Jim Casey, who sold him to Alexander, a trader	
Cesar		
Jesse		
Quaco		
Boy (Charles)		
Tina		
Rose		
Bob		
Wan		
Diana		
Hester		
Fanny		
Lizzy		
Frederick		
Rina		
Peggy		
Bella		
Judy		
John		
Polly		
Amy		
Davis		
Jim		
Rofin		
Dolly		
Eliza		
Dewitt		
Jack Bowlegs		
Beck		
Maria		
John		
Fanny		
Jenny	Sold	
Fay		
Leah		
Liddy	Sold to Dick Toney	
John	Sold to John Smith	
Latty	Eufala Tusteenuggee	
Hester	Eufala Tusteenggee	
Ben		
Molly		
Caty		
Nancy		
Israell		
Betty		
Milay		

Sam Mills		
Toney Philpot		
Dinah		
Joni		
Tom		
Mary		
Thursday		
Linda		
Hester		
Nancy		
Wannah [2]		Wife and children to Sam Mills (including Daphney, Andrew, Limus and Sarah)
Daphney		
Andrew		
Limus		In possession of Osias Hardridge.
Sarah		In possession of Osias Hardridge.

Captured Negro prisons of war Sent to Tampa Bay for freedom and Emigration to the West
From 25 Cong., 3 Sess., *Executive Document 225*, pp. 74-78

List C

Name	Est. Age	Sex	Remarks
Negroes			
Jack Bowlegs	36 years	Male	
Nancy	30 years	Female	Wife to Jack
Sancho	8 years	Male	Son to Nancy
Harriet	6 years	Female	Daughter to Nancy
Fanny	4 years	Female	Daughter to Nancy
Joe	2 years	Male	Son to Nancy
Diana	35 years	Female	Wife to Sam Bowlegs
Hester	18 years	Female	Daughter to Diana
Fanny	15 years	Female	Daughter to Diana
Lizzy	9 years	Female	Daughter to Diana
Frederick	7 years	Male	Son to Diana
Rhina	6 years	Female	Child to Diana
Peggy	5 years	Female	Child to Diana
Bella	3 years	Female	Child to Diana
Possy	60 years	Male	
Fanny	34 years	Female	Wife to Possy
Elsy	20 years	Female	Daughter to Fanny
Jenny	19 years	Female	Daughter to Fanny
Fay	18 years	Male	Son to fanny
Leah	15 years	Female	Daughter to Fanny
Liddy	10 years	Female	Daughter to Fanny
Lotty	9 years	Female	Daughter to Fanny
Hester	3 years	Female	Daughter to Fanny
Dick	25 years	Male	Husband to Elsey
Ben	5 years	Male	Son to Elsey
Molly	3 years	Female	Daughter to Elsey
Judy	1 year	Female	Daughter to Elsey
Winny	9 months	Female	Daughter to Jenny
Ned	40 years	Male	
Maria	28 years	Female	Wife to Ned
Polly	11 years	Female	Daughter to Maria
Amy	10 years	Female	Daughter to Maria
Davy	7 years	Male	Son to Maria
Rophile	5 years	Male	Son to Maria
Jim	4 years	Male	Son to Maria
Charles	60 years	Male	
Katy	40 years	Female	Wife to Charles

Jim	21 years	Male	Son to Katy
Nancy	24 years	Female	Daughter to Katy
Hardy	26 years	Male	Husband to Nancy
Sally	2 years	Female	Daughter to Nancy
Plenty	37 years	Male	
Rose	35 years	Female	Wife to Plenty
Wan	15 years	Male	Son to Rose
Jack	13 years	Male	Son to Rose
Sally	12 years	Female	Daughter to Rose
Rachae1	1l years	Female	Daughter to Rose
Caesar	7 years	Male	Son to Rose
Jesse	6 years	Male	Son to Rose
Jesse	22 years	Male	Brother to Plenty
Nancy	37 years	Female	Sister to Plenty
Bacchus	20 years	Male	Son to Nancy
Sue	18 years	Female	Daughter to Nancy
Thomas	3 years	Male	Son to Nancy
Carolina	34 years	Male	Brother to Plenty
Teenar	28 years	Female	Wife to Carolina
Rose	5 years	Female	Daughter to Teenar
Bob	4 years	Male	Son to Teenar
Rophile	36 years	Male	
Hetty	33 years	Female	Wife to Rophile
Belinda	15 years	Female	Daughter to Hetty
Nancy	14 years	Female	Daughter to Hetty
Rose	12 years	Female	Daughter to Hetty
Sarah Ann	11 years	Female	Daughter to Hetty
Straffar	9 years	Male	Son to Hetty
Primus	60 years	Male	
Sandy	65 years	Male	
Lucy	55 years	Female	Wife to Sandy
Hernar	36 years	Female	Daughter to Lucy
Rose	21 years	Female	Daughter to Lucy
Hannah	19 years	Female	Daughter to Lucy
Elsy	16 years	Female	Daughter to Lucy
Thomas	14 years	Male	Son to Lucy
Dembo	30 years	Male	Son to Lucy
Juby	40 years	Male	Husband to Hernar
Suzy	19 years	Female	Daughter to Hernar
Nanny	17 years	Female	Daughter to Hernar
Sanson	14 years	Male	Son to Hernar
Nelly	12 years	Female	Daughter to Hernar
Kistoba	9 years	Male	Son to Hernar
Jenny	5 years	Female	Daughter to Hernar
Mag	2 years	Female	Daughter to Rose
Jack	70 years	Male	
Sarah	55 years	Female	Wife to Jack
Taymour	27 years	Female	Daughter to Sarah

Ishmael	25 years Male	Son to Sarah
Phebe	23 years Female	Daughter to Sarah
Cosar	20 years Male	Son to Sarah
Peggy	18 years Female	Daughter to Sarah
Charles (or Tenebo)	34 years Male	Husband to Taymour
Hagar	8 years Female	Daughter to Taymour
Pussy	6 years Female	Daughter to Taymour
Harriet	4 years Female	Daughter to Taymour
Hernar	7 years Female	Daughter to Phebe
Ned	5 years Male	Son to Phebe
Old John	60 years Male	
Flora	50 years Female	Wife to Old John
Jim	25 years Male	Son to Flora
Rose	23 years Female	Daughter to Flora
Milly	21 years Female	Daughter to Flora
William	20 years Male	Son to Flora
Hannah	18 years Female	Daughter to Flora
Cosar	15 years Male	Son to Flora
Eve	14 years Female	Daughter to Flora
Dolly	12 years Female	Daughter to Flora
Sam	11 years Male	Son to Flora
Phillis	10 years Female	Daughter to Flora
Jeffrey	6 years Male	Son to Flora
Milly	3 years Female	Daughter to Flora
John	25 years Male	Husband to Rose
Betsey	6 years Female	Daughter to Rose
Joe	5 years Male	Son to Rose
Titus	2 years Male	Son to Rose
Tom	24 years Male	Husband to Milly
Ben	5 years Male	Son to Milly
Judy	3 years Female	Daughter to Milly
Sam	53 years Male	Brother to Flora
Judy	22 years Female	Wife to Jim

Captured Negroes   Meant to Emigrate to the West but who were Prevented by Sickness from Accompanying Those in

List C

From 25 Cong., 3 Sess., *Executive Document 225*, p. 79

List D

Name	Age	Sex	Remarks

Negroes

Sam Bowlegs	30 years Male	Retained to act as interpreter
Scipio	28 years Male	Brother to Sam
Bess	30 years Female	Wife to Scipio
Hard Times	10 years Male	Son to Bess
Took-hear	9 years Female	Daughter to Bess
Porris	8 years Male	Son to Bess
John	7 years Male	Son to Bess
Black	6 years Male	Son to Bess
Long Bob	45 years Male	
Flora	33 years Female	Wife to Long Bob
Eve	15 years Female	Daughter to Flora
Jenny	6 years Female	Daughter to Flora
Beck	36 years Female	Husband went off with Jumper
Maria	14 years Female	Daughter to Beck

Negroes prisoners of war Turned Over by Lieut. Terrett, 9ᵗʰ April 1838

From National Archives Record Group 75, Records of the Bureau of Indian Affairs, Miscellaneous *Muster Rolls, 1832-1846:* Seminole.

List E

Name		Sex	Remarks
Plenty		Male	
Rose		Female	
Sally	Child		
Rachael	Child		
Caesar	Child		
Jesse	Child		
Wan	Child		Died at N.O. 17ᵗʰ May
Jack	Child		
Jesse		Male	
Rufile or Rafail		Male	
Hetty		Female	
Belinden	Child		
Nancy	Child		
Rose	Child		
Sarah Ann	Child		
Staffer	Child		
Eliza		Female	

Mary	Child		
Ledora	Child		
Mungo	Child		
Pussey		Female	
Cumba	Child		
Lindy	Child		
Latty		Male	
Old Peter		Male	
Teena		Female	
Primus		Male	
Scipio		Male	
Daphne		Female	
Katy		Female	
Stephen			
Hackly		Male	
Fanny		Female	Died on board the steamer *South Alabama* 29th May
Elsy		Female	
Jenny		Female	
Leah		Female	
Fay		Male	
John	Child		
Lydia	Child		
Lotty	Child		
Esther	Child		
Ben	Child		
Molly	Child		
Judy	Child		
Winny	Child		
Dick		Male	
Jane		Female	Died on board the steamer *South Alabama* 3rd June
Sylla		Female	
Charles		Male	
Abram		Male	
Flora		Female	Detained at N.O. by the Civil Authority
Abbey		Female	Detained at N.O. by the Civil Authority
Jack		Male	
Nancy		Female	
Sanko	Child		
Harriet	Child		Died on board

170

Name			Remarks
			the steamer *South Alabama* 26th May
Fanny	Child		
Joe	Child		
Old John		Male	
Flora		Female	
William		Male	
Annah		Female	
Caesar		Male	
Milly		Female	
Eve	Child		
Sam	Child		
Phyllis	Child		
Jeffrey	Child		
Milley	Child		
Ben	Child		
Rudy	Child		
Old Sam		Male	
Peter Jumper		Male	
Hannah		Female	
Tom		Male	
Friday		Male	
Ned	Child		
Fanny	Child		
Alexander or Allick	Child		
Daniel	Child		
Clara	Child		
Charles		Male	Died on board steamer *South Alabama* 2nd June
Katy		Female	
Jim		Male	
Nancy		Female	
Judy		Female	
Hardy		Male	

Negroes Turned Over by Lieut. Mack U.S.A., 11th May 1838

From National Archives Record Group 75, Records of the Bureau of Indian Affairs, Miscellaneous *Muster Rolls, 1832-1846:* Seminole.

List F

Name	Remarks

Scipio		Delia
Bessy or Bess	Died on board	Fanny
	the steamer *South*	Bella
	Alabama 2nd June	Lucy
Hardtimes		Adam
Poros		Toney
Tuckya		Towsdey
John		Dinah
Black		Caty
Esther		Jinney
Romeo		Sarah
Cilla		Tepney
Peter		Tom
Ceasar		Lucy
William		Sam
Aaron		Possey
Edsey		Diana
Hetty		Hester
Silla		Fanny
Pompey		Jim
Billey		Lizzy
Bob		Frederick
Primus		Rhina
Hagar		Peggy
		Bella

Negroes prisoner of war Received at Tampa Bay

From National Archives Record Group 75, Records of the Bureau of Indian Affairs, Miscellaneous *Muster Rolls, 1832-1846:* Seminole.

List G[3]

Name	Sex	Remarks
Sandy	Male	
Dambo	Male	
Betsy	Female	
Eve	Female	
Nancy	Female	
Jane	Female	
Plenty	Male	
Lucy	Female	
Anna	Female	
Johnson	Male	
Ester	Female	
York	Male	

172

Timus	Male
Nelson	Male
Peter	Male
Thomas	Male
Elky	Female
Hannah	Female
Lybby	Female
Aphy	Female
Rose	Female
Mikey	Female
Sandy	Male
Cuffy	Male
Pompey	Male
Robert	Male
Lucy	Female
Abby	Female
Suky	Female
Flora	Female
Bayal	Female
Carolina	Female
Eve	Female
Clara	Female
Carolina	Female
Sam	Male
Eliza	Female
Pussey	Female
Thomas	Male
Rose	Female
Robert	Male
Jim	Male
Easter	Female	Died on board the steamer *South Alabama* 26th May
Bessy	Female
Ester	Female
Margaret	Female
Titus	Male
Cuffy	Male
Rose	Female
Teena	Female
Wanna	Female
Sarah	Female
Peggy	Female
Jack	Male
Peggy	Female
Ismael	Male
Phoeby	Female
Nat	Male

Harriet	Female
Hagar	Female
Pussey	Female
Thomas	Female
Caesar	Male
Cornelia	Female
Pompey	Male
Jackson	Male
Maria	Female
Beck	Female
Tanneba	Female
Robert	Female
Hector	Female

List of Refugees and Captured African belonging to the Seminole nation
From 25 Cong., 3 Sess., House Document 225, pp. 95-96.

List H

Name	Age	Remarks
Peter, first	45 years	
Peter, second	45 years	
Tom	55 years	
Sam	46 years	
Lancaster	28 years	
Morris	27 years	
Sampson	25 years	
Joe, first	23 years	
Andrew	21 years	
Dick	40 years	
Hardy	25 years	
Worley	28 years	
Ansel	24 years	
Israel	20 years	
Jim	18 years	Brother to Israel
Cyrus	16 years	
Mungo	45 years	
Joe, second	25 years	
Cornelia	55 years	Mother to Lancaster, Morris, Sampson, Joe (first), Andrew, and Dick
Caty, first	60 years	Wife to Tom
Jane	40 years	Mother to Cyrus, Stepney, and Affy

174

Dolly	35 years	Wife to Sam
Sophy	28 years	Wife to Morris
Beck	28 years	Wife to Lancaster
Amy	28 years	Wife to Peter (first), and mother to Nancy, Lymus, York, and Hester
Nancy	24 years	Wife to Hardy
Hagar	24 years	Daughter to Peggy and mother to Philip
Peggy	40 years	Mother to Hagar
Pamilla	45 years	Enticed away by an Indian who has her as his wife
Caty, second	24 years	Wife of Sampson
Lydia	35 years	
Nancy	8 years	Child to Peter (first) and Amy
Lymus	6 years	Child to Peter (first) and Amy
York	4 years	Child to Peter (first) and Amy
Hester	2 years	Child to Peter (first) and Amy
Cooter	9 years	Child to Peter Lancaster and Beck
Tom	7 years	Child to Peter Lancaster and Beck
Frank	5 years	Child to Peter Lancaster and Beck
A girl	2 years	Child to Peter Lancaster and Beck
Stepney	7 years	Child to Jane
Affy	5 years	Child to Jane
Cyrus	5 years	Child to Sampson
Elsey	4 years	Child to Sampson
Philip	5 years	Child to Hagar
Caty, third	50 years	Mother to Nancy, Israel, and Jim

List of Seminole Negro Prisoners of war of Lieut. J. G. Reynolds, March 21ˢᵗ 1838

From National Archives Record Group 75, Records of the Bureau of Indian Affairs, *Miscellaneous Muster Rolls, 1832-1846*: Seminole.

List I

Name	Sex	Age	Remarks
Prince	Male	32 years	Detained at N.O. by the Civil Authority
Noble	Male	25 years	Detained at N.O. by the Civil Authority
Monday	Male	25 years	
Primus	Male	30 years	
Dick	Male	58 years	
Ben	Male	40 years	
Joe	Male	25 years	
Bunno	Male	18 years	
Wann 1st	Male	75 years	
Toby	Male	45 years	
Dailey	Male	18 years	Detained at N.O. by the Civil Authority
Toney	Male	45 years	Detained at N.O. by the Civil Authority
Jacob 1st	Male	39 years	
Jacob 2nd	Male	29 years	Detained at N.O. by the Civil Authority
Lewis	Male	55 years	Detained at N.O. by the Civil Authority
Sand 2nd	Male	40 years	
Sand 1st	Male	60 years	
Carolina	Male	35 years	
Israel	Male	25 years	
Peter	Male	70 years	
Wann 2nd	Male	30 years	Detached for Tampa Bay 19th April by order Of General Jesup
Ned	Male	20 years	Detached for Tampa Bay 19th April by order Of General Jesup
Kibbitt	Male	25 years	
Fanny	Female	25 years	Detained at N.O. by the Civil Authority
Juda	Female	30 years	Detained at N.O. by the Civil Authority
Hagah	Female	26 years	Detained at N.O. by the Civil Authority
Katty 1st	Female	35 years	Detained at N.O. by the Civil Authority
Katty 2nd	Female	35 years	Detained at N.O. by the Civil Authority

Eliza 1st	Female	60 years	
Eliza 2nd	Female	28 years	Detained at N.O. by the Civil Authority
Jean 1st	Female	60 years	
Jean 2nd	Female	28 years	
Silla	Female	35 years	Detained at N.O. by the Civil Authority
Tunee	Female	58 years	Detained at N.O. by the Civil Authority
Dollie	Female	75 years	Detained at N.O. by the Civil Authority
Elsy	Female	26 years	Died at New Orleans 18th April
Patty 1st	Female	30 years	Detained at N.O. by the Civil Authority
Patty 2nd	Female	33 years	One female child born 30th April
Flora	Female	10 years	
Molley	Female	12 years	Detained at N.O. by the Civil Authority
Rinee	Female	35 years	
Mary	Female	22 years	Detained at N.O. by the Civil Authority
Rose	Female	30 years	Died on board the steamer *South Alabama* 31st May
Peggy	Female	70 years	Detained at N.O. by the Civil Authority
Suza	Female	55 years	One birth to a female child 11th May
Linda	Female	45 years	
Nancy	Female	10 years	
Pussey	Female	12 years	Detained at N.O. by the Civil Authority
Sue	Female	16 years	
Lucy	Female	10 years	
Bessy	Female	50 years	
Wanna	Female	40 years	
Millie	Female	18 years	
Polly	Female	15 years	Died at N. Orleans 20th of May
Daphney	Female	9 years	
Lidia	Female	25 years	
Billy	Male	14 years	Detained at N.O. by the Civil Authority
Johnny	Male	7 years	
Toney	Male	14 years	

Name	Sex	Age	Remarks
Thomas	Male	12 years	Detained at N.O. by the Civil Authority
Charles 1st	Male	9 years	
Charles 2nd	Male	8 years	Detained at N.O. by the Civil Authority
Ishmael	Male	8 years	Detained at N.O. by the Civil Authority
Argus	Male	12 years	
Pompey	Male	6 years	
Scipio 1st	Male	5 years	
Lyrus	Male	5 years	Detained at N.O. by the Civil Authority
Scipio 2nd	Male	1 ½ years	Detained at N.O. by the Civil Authority
Sandy	Male	3 years	
March	Male	14 years	
Doc	Male	9 years	
Andrew at the breast	Male		
Betty	Female	4 years	
Tamour	Female	3 years	Detained at N.O. by the Civil Authority
Elsy	Female	3 years	
Fanny	Female	4 years	Detained at N.O. by the Civil Authority
Katty	Female	5 years	
Silba	Female	2 years	The remark applied to Margaret also exists to Silba, being about one year old
Margaret	Female	10 years	Left at N.O. by Lieut. Reynolds (with her Mother) in conse quence of youth, being about three years old instead of ten as here required
Venus	Female	6 years	
Matilda	Female	4 years	
Catherine	Female	5 years	
Bella	Female	12 years	Detained at N.O. by the Civil Authority
Patty	Female	4 years	

List of African prisoners of war who were part of the Seminole Nation April 19, 1835[4].

From National Archives Microfilm Publications, *Microcopy M234*, Roll 802, Seminole D 153-56.

List J

Names and Comments

Pompey, an old man
His wife Dolly with children and grand children as follows
Ned, a man
Bob, a man
Primus, a man
Nancy, with her youngest child
Silla, with two children, Tom and Bella
Caty
Nelly, with children Scippio and Sandy
Fanny, with children Charles and Margarett
Eliza
Boner, a boy, son of Nancy
Sancho, a boy, son of Nancy
Harriett, girl, daughter of Nancy
Jeane, oldest daughter of Pompey by former wife
John
Isaac
Toney
Pompey
Jack
Molly and child Billy
Susey
Riner and her child Venus
Old Tenah, her children and grand children as follows:
George
Monday
Sampson
Peter
Elsey and her child Caty
Patty and her three children Lucy, Pompey, and small one Matilla
Mary and her four children Pompey, Ismael, Cyrus, and Tayman
Sally and her child
Susey
Nancy
Linda
John, and old man, with his wife
Flora and their children and grand children as follows:
Jim
William
Caesar
Sam
Rose, with her children Betsy and Joe
Milly and her child Ben

Hannah
Dolly
Fillis
Jeffrey
Eaph
Peggy, with children and grand children as follows:
Joe
Hagar and her children Phillis and Ned

List of Negroes Who Surrendered Under Major General Jesup's Proclamation

From National Archives Microfilms Publications, *Microcopy M574*, Roll 13, Special File 96: Seminole Claims to Certain negroes, 1841-1849.

List K

Name	Remarks
August	
Jno. Cowaya (Gopher John)	
Old Peter	
Tina	Dead
Pompey	
Primus	
Dephney	
Caty	Also daughter Fanny
Matilda	Absent
Rat	
Paris	Dead
Cyrus	
John	
Sylla	Dead
Old Charles	Free
Hannah	Also daughters Fanny and Sylla and son Peter
Old Simon	Free
Clary	
Elsey and child Dolly	
Ben	
Hetty	Sold to Dick Stinson, who sold her
Billy	Augusts' sons, present
Bob	Sold to John Drew
Peter, a big man	Dead
Cuffy	
Sukey	

Jim
Colly
Cesar
Aaron
Titus
Pompey
Calina
Thomas
Pussy
Eliza
Rosa
Sam
Sarah
Armstrong
Eliza   August's wife
Mary   August's child
Mungo   August's child
Tina
Abbey
Easther   Dead
Marguerette
Robbin
Jim
Betsy
Freeman
Rabbit (Friday)
Buck
Aleck
Daniel   Dead
Clary
Latty   Sold
Dindy
Cumba
Romeo   Mr. Dupeister paid for him by
                                                Congress
Lidda
Kivet
Patty
Latty
Flora
Jane
Silla   Children: Mungo, Katy, Latty
                                                and Jane
Abraham
Cuffy
Hager
Boston

Renty	
Adam	
Lucy	
Quash or Quasse	
Delia	
Harkless	
Sarah	
Pompey	
Wann	Absent in Texas
Cornelia	2 children, Pompey and Isaac
Jim	
Sandy	Free
Nanny	
John	
Tina	
Betsy and child Suky	
Sylla and child Plenty	
Affy and child Mary	
Silvia	
Eve	
Judy	Dead
John Wan	
Molly	
Phie	
Nancy and child Rose	
Sam Jane	
Bachhus	Dead
Kitty	
Bob	
Peter	Free
Hardy	
Amy	
Nessey	Sold to Hill, a trader in the Indian country
Limey	
York	
Johnston	
Peggy	Dead
Jack	Dead
July	Killed in Florida
Tina and her 2 children, Hannah and Julia	
Susan	
Nanny	2 children: Cuffee and Kibbett
Nelly and child Murray	
Sampson	
Kistova	

Jenny	
Noretta	
Pond	No such person
Rosenti	
Robert	
Kuntessee	No such person
Phillis	Dead
Joe	
Sundy	Dead
Lucy	Free
Dembo	
Thomas	
Elsey and child Rachel	
Rose	Absent at Little River
Mike	Absent at Little River
Hannah	Absent at Little River
Frank	
July Jr.	Dead
Liddy	
Sandy	Dead
Hetty	
Rofile	Free
Linda	
Nancy	
Rode	
Sarah	
Traphom	
Lewis	
Nancy	
Bacchus	
Susan	
Thomas	
Jessee	
Monday	
Tom	
Old Primus	
Flora	
Queen	Bob and Hetty
Abia	
Sarah	Dead
Jack	
Dick	
Ismael	
Peggy	
Tamar	
March	
Kokee	

Hagar	
Pussy	
Dosha	
Harriet	
Tennibo	Dead
Long Bob	Dead
Old John	
Flora	
William	
Jim	
Rose	
Milly	
Caesar	
Eve	
Phillis	
Jeffrey	Dead
Milly	
Nanny	
Betsey	
Joe	Dead
Titus	
Williams	Dead
Cudjo	Dead
Ben	
Rudy	
Jim	
Charlotte	Dead
Harriett	
Hannah	Dead
Nancy	
Sancho	
Fanny	
Prince	Dead
Ned	
Ned 2nd	
Jack	
Rose and child John	
Plenty	Dead
Sally and child Joe	
Rachel	
Jack	Free
Caesar	Sold him to Jim Carey, who sold him to Alexander, a trader
Cuffee	Free
Jessee	
Quaco	
Boy (Charles)	

Tina	
Rose	
Bob	
Wan	
Diana	Dead
Hester	3 children: Vina, Dinda, and Colly
Fanny	
Frederick	
Lirry	
Rina	
Peggy	
Bella	
Judy	Burnt up at Deep Fork
John	
Polly	
Amy	Dead
Davis	
Jim	
Rofile	
Dolly	
Eliza	
Dewitt	
Jack Bowlegs	
Beck	
Maria	
John	
Fanny	Dead
Tenny	
Fay	
Leah and child Lizzy	
Liddy	Sold to Dick Toney
John	Sold to John Smith
Latty	
Hester	
Ben	
Molly	
Caty	
Nancy	Claimed by Mrs. Leonard
Israel	Run off by traders
Betty	
Milay	Sold in Cherokee Nation
Sam Mills	Free
Toney Philpot	
Dinah	
Dice	Dead
Tom	

Mary	
Thursday	
Linda	
Hester	Dead
Nancy	
Limas	Sold and run off
Sarah	Sold and run off
Wannah	
Dephney	
Katey	
Andrew	
Washington	
Hannah	
Joe	
Mary	
Flora	
July	
Dolly	
Adam	
Lucy	
Dinda	Dead
Rabbit	
Fay	
Peggy	
Colby	
Scilla	
Toney	
Pussy	
Ned	
Abraham	
Andrew	
Jesse	
Mary	
Levi	
Isaac	Dead
Judy	
Jim	
Jane	
Harkless	
Wally	
Pomilla	
Sarah	

List of captured Negroes said to Belonging to the Seminole Nation

From National Archives Microfilms Publications, *Microcopy M234*,
Roll 802, Seminole D 153-56.

List L[55] This list was apparently made by Marcellus Duval in 1849; it
was taken from a certified copy of the original, which was in the
hands of Halleck Tustenuggee in 1855. Compare it with List J.

Name	Remarks
Old John	
Flora	
Jim	
Rose	
Milla	
William	
Hannah	
Caesar	
Eve	
Sam	
Phillis	
Jeffrey	
Jeffrey	
Ben	
Rose	
Betsy	
Titus	
Elsy	Sold
Toby	Sold
Monday	
Nancy	
Linder	Sold
Susy	
Jonny	
Samson	
Patty	
Lucy	
Pompey	
Martilla	
Pussee	Sold
Silas	
Scipio	
Tamar	
Ismeal	Issue do not Belong
Caty	
Fanny	
Eliza	Sold
Caty	Sold

Name	Status
Cillee	Sold
Nancy	
Nelly	
Bones	
Sanco	
Fanny	Sold
Thomas	Sold
Margaret	
Sylvia	
Scipio	
Sandy	
Hagar	Issue do not Belong
Sampson	
Isaac	
Jack	
Sary	
Molly	
Riner	
Venus	
Billy	
Pompey	
Ned	Sold
Bob	
Sampson	
Charles	
John	
Small Girl	Daughter of Riner
Son of Sarah	

ENDNOTES:

[1] Apparently a mistake, the description fits Juan.

[2] Wannah, Daphney , Andrew, Limus, and Sarah: these names are written in Jesup's handwriting and were probably added in 1845, when Jesup was at Fort Gibson; at that time Limus and Sarah were in Hardridge's possession. A further notation in Jesup's hand reads, "Holatoochee (asking the only way possible to protect his captured Negro comrades from enslavement got jussup to promise the captured Negro Warrior be kept by him under the only title acceptable to the Anglo American Conquers "slaves", but they were never to be sold or separated and were to be ultimately free. This was understood to be with their own consent. Those Negroes are recorded to have said "That chief who rendered us important services is now dead."

[3] A note on the list reads, "One female Child Born 20th March, died 28th May."

[4]   This list was sworn to on April 24, 1835, by Coa Hajo, Billy Hicks, and Hotulsee Emathla, who said they were council at Big Swamp after the death of chief Tuskenehau, when the council decreed that these Africans were deem to be the property of Miccopotokee or Copiah Yahola. However, testimony subsequently to this date indicates that Miccopotokee received the Africans as guardian for Tuskenehau's daughters. Compare this list to List L. On the back of the list appear the following notes:

    "Caty - Assil's daughter;
    Eve - Cuffy's child,
    Fanny – Big Frances' sister;
    Sylvia – Big Frances' daughter;
    Jack Bowlegs – Big Frances' husband;
    Venus – Riner's daughter;
    Lucy – Pompey's daughter, Jim's wife, child of Venus;
    Sampson – Tiner's son;
    Phillis – Blind John's daughter;
    Sandy, run off;
    Sarah – Primus' wife."

CONTRIBUTORS

Cornelia Bailey is an Elder of the Gullah-Geechee Nation, and great-great-great-granddaughter of Bilali, among the most celebrated of the first captured African Muslims in America.

Rodger Lyle Brown holds a Ph.D. in southern studies from Emory University and is the author of *Ghost Dancing on the Cracker Circuit: The Culture of Festivals in the American South* and *Party Out of Bounds: The B-52's, R.E.M. and the Kids Who Rocked Athens, Ga.* He is a former managing editor of Encyclopedia Britannica's website Britannica.com and has written for *The New York Times Magazine, Fortune, The Atlanta Journal/Constitution* and numerous other publications.

J. Vern Cromartie is Professor of Sociology at Contra Costa College in California.

Y. N. Kly is Professor Emeritus at the School of Human Justice, University of Regina, Saskatchewan, Canada. His works include, *International Law and the Black Minority in the U.S.* and *A Popular Guide to Minority Rights,* both of which were awarded the Gustavus Myers Center for Human Rights "Outstanding Book" Award, in 1990 and 1995 respectively. He is presently Chair and founder of IHRAAM, an international NGO in consultative status with the United Nations.

Carlie Towne is an Elder of the Gullah-Geechee Nation, a Member of its Wisdom Council, and Director of the Gullah-Geechee Foundation.

Peter H. Wood is professor of history at Duke University, and author, inter alia, of *The Black Majority:Negroes in Colonial South Carolina from 1670 Through the Stono Rebellion* and *Strange New Land: African Americans, 1526-1776.* He was awarded a Rhodes Scholarship in 1964, research fellowships from Harvard's Charles Warren Center (1974-75), the Guggenheim Foundation (1975 for 1976-77), and the National Endowment for the Humanities (1975-77). He received the Albert J. Beveridge Award (1974) and the James Harvey Robinson Prize (1984) of the American Historical Association. In 2002, he delivered the Lamar Memorial Lectures at Mercer University in Macon, GA. Prof. Wood holds a Ph.D. from Harvard University.

INDEX

LEADERS
of the
SEMINOLE WARS

ABRAHAM / IBRAHIM

JOHN HORSE / JUAN CAVALLO

25051327R00113

Printed in Great Britain
by Amazon